Colin Spencer is one of the best known vegetarian authors in Britain today. He writes a regular column on vegetarian cookery in the *Guardian* Newspaper and has published a number of vegetarian cookbooks, including *Good and Healthy* (published in paperback as *Colin Spencer's Vegetarian and Wholefood Book*) and *Cordon Vert*. He lives in the country and grows many of his own vegetables, insuring the finest flavors for the vegetarian recipes he develops. He is also the author of nine novels and is a talented painter.

Dr. Tom Sanders is Lecturer in Nutrition at King's College, University of London, and a recognized authority on vegetarianism. He has researched and written many papers on vegetarian diets. His other special areas of interest are diet-related heart disease and young children's diets. He has appeared on a number of radio and television programs concerned with nutrition.

The Vegetarian Kitchen

A Natural Program for Health & Nutrition

Colin Spencer and Tom Sanders, Ph.D.

Foreword by
Fredrick J. Stare, M.D.
Professor of Nutrition, Emeritus
Harvard School of Public Health

THE BODY PRESS

To Linda, Mila and Toby

TS

Publisher: Rick Bailey
Executive Editor: Sam Mitnick
Editor: Patricia J. Aaron

The Body Press, a division of HPBooks, Inc.
P.O. Box 5367
Tucson, AZ 85703
(602) 888-2150

Library of Congress Cataloging-in-Publication Data

Spencer, Colin.
  The vegetarian kitchen.

  Includes index.
  1. Vegetarianism.   2. Vegetarian cookery.
I. Sanders, Tom, Ph. D.   II. Title.
RM 236.S64   1986   641.5'636   86–26919
ISBN 0-89586-467-3

1st Printing

Photoset in 10 point Garamond by
𝍫 Tek Art Limited, Croydon, England

Notice: The information in this book is true and complete to the best of our knowledge. All recommendations are made without guarantees on the part of the authors or HPBooks. The authors and publishers disclaim all liability in connection with the use of this information.

First published in Great Britain in 1986
by Martin Dunitz Limited,
154 Camden High Street,
London NW1 0NE

CONTENTS

FOREWORD

Some years ago, when I was Chairman of the Department of Nutrition at Harvard School of Public Health, I learned about vegetarianism from a few graduate students who were ovo-lactovegetarians and who did their doctorate theses on vegetarianism. Our first research paper on vegetarianism was published in the *Journal of Clinical Nutrition* in 1954.

Health advantages that ovo-lactovegetarians have over most people who include meat in their diets include: lower body weight, lower levels of cholesterol in the blood, and appreciably more fiber in their diets.

The strict vegetarian, the vegan, has a difficult time maintaining good health. Adequate iron, protein of superior nutritional quality, and vitamin B_{12} are not readily available, particularly the last since it is present mainly in foods of animal origin.

Dr. Tom Sanders in his introduction to *The Vegetarian Kitchen* has done an excellent job explaining the scientific and nutritional basis of vegetarianism.

Colin Spencer has some helpful Cooking Hints, some very attractive colored photos and, according to my wife who is a gourmet cook and who has tried some of the recipes, dishes that are tasty and delicious.

I recommend this book highly to those who wish to be accurately informed about vegetarianism.

Fredrick J. Stare, M.D.
Professor of Nutrition, Emeritus
Harvard School of Public Health

INTRODUCTION

There has been a staggering increase in the number of vegetarians in Western countries over the past twenty years so that it is now commonplace to hear people asking for vegetarian food in restaurants, hotels and even airplanes. What is often a problem for new vegetarians or their relatives is whether their diet will be adequate. Is there a danger of protein or vitamin and mineral deficiencies? Is there an increased risk of anemia? Are there any dangers for young children or pregnant and nursing mothers? Although a considerable amount of scientific research has been carried out over the past ten years looking into the diets and health of vegetarians, the answers to these questions have not been easily available. Our intention is to provide a clear guide on how to follow a sound, appetizing and yet a simple to prepare vegetarian diet. We hope this book will be useful not only to new vegetarians and those trying out vegetarian food part-time, but also to those who find following their principles among meat eaters sometimes inconvenient, so that they are inclined to rely on snacks of salty cheese or peanuts rather than bother to prepare proper meals.

Why are so many people turning to vegetarianism? There are currently many vegetarians in the US and many more who eat some meals without meat. Fifty years ago the idea was considered strange and only for religious sects or fringe groups. People decide to give up eating meat for different reasons – for religious or moral convictions, for health, or to support the economic and ecological arguments. Often it seems to be a combination of all these or just a wish to experiment with another way of eating that leads people into vegetarianism. How long they remain vegetarian depends on the strength of their convictions and whether they like the food.

It is easy to choose a diet that is high in fat, salt and sugar – not a recipe for good health. Now that there has been so much publicity about eating healthfully, vegetarians need to consider how they should follow the recommended guidelines. In this book we show ways of following a balanced diet that make vegetarian eating both healthful and a pleasure. Each recipe gives an analysis of its calorie, protein, fat, carbohydrate and fiber content. By combining this information with the advice we give here, you can plan attractive and nutritious vegetarian meals.

WHAT ARE THE REASONS FOR BEING VEGETARIAN?

Most people become vegetarian because they abhor animal suffering and find eating meat repulsive. Many also believe that a vegetarian diet is more natural and wholesome than the typical Western diet and therefore more healthful. This idea owes a lot to the food reform lobby who, in the mid-nineteenth century, showed that many foods were over-refined and adulterated with chemicals. Meat products were also often contaminated. They recommended a diet based on whole grain cereals, fruit, vegetables and fresh milk. The distinction today is of course less clear-cut. Because a vegetarian diet is often prescribed by practitioners of alternative medicine, orthodox medical practitioners are sometimes suspicious of the health claims made for vegetarianism.

Another current reason for giving up meat is that a vegetarian diet is more economical when taken in the context of limited food resources which are becoming a worldwide concern. Most of the cereal crop grown in developed countries is used to feed farm animals, yet these cereals could be used directly for human consumption. Producing meat is an inefficient way of feeding people; it takes about ten pounds of cereals to produce one pound of beef. Cereals could be diverted from animal production to feed the hungry in developing countries.

Historically, vegetarianism has strong religious links and this is still the inspiration for a large proportion of vegetarians. In many cultures it was believed that the consumption of flesh would contaminate the mind with thoughts of pleasures of the flesh. This is why vegetarianism has been associated with asceticism and purity of thought. The Hindu and Sikh religions advocate a vegetarian diet, as do certain Muslim and Christian sects. Vegetarianism has also been associated with radical movements, such as pacifism, Fabianism, feminism and animal liberation.

A lot of people are turning vegetarian, if not exclusively, at least for a major part of their diet, because of the new attraction of the foods. In the past, vegetarian diets were usually monotonous. Now, with changes in communications and food technology, many fruits and vegetables can be bought year-round so that vegetarian diets can be extremely varied.

DIFFERENT TYPES OF VEGETARIAN DIETS

Vegetarianism covers a broad range of diets. All vegetarians exclude meat and fish; a lactovegetarian includes milk and its products; an ovo-vegetarian includes eggs; an ovo-lactovegetarian diet includes both eggs and milk products; a vegan or strict vegetarian diet contains no food of animal origin whatsoever; a fruitarian diet, which is the most extreme or ultimate form, consists only of raw fruit, nuts and berries.

Usually the first stage in becoming a vegetarian is to give up eating red meat and this is followed by excluding poultry and fish. Some vegetarians give up cows' milk and its products (butter, cheese, yogurt) because they believe that milk production is cruel; calves are taken away from their mothers and are either artificially reared or killed for veal so that the cows' milk can be used for human consumption. Others argue that it was intended for calves, not man, and having cows' milk is unnatural. Some vegetarians object to eating eggs for similar reasons. The majority of vegetarians want intensive farming abolished, especially the "battery" conditions for egg-producing chickens. Most of those who eat them buy free-range eggs.

Vegans reject all food of animal origin, including milk and its products, eggs, honey and food that has been processed using animal products. Vegans do not use animal products for other purposes. They do not wear fur coats or leather shoes, or use cosmetics which either contain animal products or which have been tested on laboratory animals.

The diet of our ancestors probably consisted mainly of raw fruit, nuts and berries supplemented with odd insects and small animals. As human beings became civilized, they learned to cultivate plants and how to process certain plants, particularly cereals and root crops, into food. Fruitarians believe people can live on a diet of fruit, nuts and berries and so they exclude grains and processed foods from their diets. Some believe that it is wrong to uproot living plants. Most fruitarians previously have been vegans and most vegans in turn have been vegetarians. Fruitarianism is part of the same philosophy as vegetarianism. Of all the vegetarian diets this is the most likely to be inadequate, as you will see.

HOW HEALTHY IS A VEGETARIAN DIET?

A common assumption – already mentioned as one of the reasons for people becoming vegetarians – is that the diet itself is more healthful than eating meat. So far this has not been proven scientifically. Conversely, people fear they or their children will become anemic or underweight. The truth is that the health of vegetarians is very similar to that of meat eaters. There are certainly aspects of the diet which are particularly healthful and those that need to be watched to insure adequate nutrition. These are explained on pages 13–22.

Several studies have tried to compare the health of vegans and vegetarians with the rest of the population but it is not easy to arrive at a clear answer. Vegetarians often show a different attitude towards health. Many are middle-class and tend not to smoke or drink. How long anyone has been a vegetarian is important, and so are the reasons for choosing to become vegetarian. People who become vegetarians for health reasons obviously bias the results of a study, especially if they started the diet with the aim of curing an illness.

The Seventh Day Adventist church advocates a vegetarian diet. Studies of the causes of death of its members have been made here in the United States. Seventh Day Adventists tend to live longer and have lower rates of death from cancer and heart disease compared with the other people studied. But they also differ in other ways: they do not smoke, drink tea, coffee or alcohol. Besides, studies of other religious groups, for example Mormons, who do not follow a vegetarian diet and do not smoke or drink, have similarly low rates of cancer and heart disease. This implies that it is not the vegetarian diet that is providing the protection.

Medical examinations made on vegetarians and vegans compared with meat eaters fail to show that they are less healthy or more prone to deficiencies, with the notable exception of vitamin B_{12} (see page 20). Vegans and vegetarians are no more likely to suffer from anemia than meat eaters. They tend to be lighter than other people of the same height. This is because they carry less fat, which is an advantage since obesity can increase the risk of conditions such as heart disease, gout and diabetes.

Protecting against heart disease
Coronary heart disease is the main cause of death among middle-aged men in the Western world. It is rare in developing countries, where less food

of animal origin is eaten, but when people from developing countries begin to eat a Western diet they soon acquire the disease. Several environmental factors have been associated with it – smoking, stress, lack of exercise and diet. It is linked to another condition called atherosclerosis, which may take twenty or thirty years to develop. The arteries become scarred and furred up with fatty material called atheroma, the Greek for porridge.

If one of the coronary arteries that supplies the heart muscle with blood becomes blocked, a heart attack is the result. The blockage is often caused by a blood clot. Atherosclerosis increases the risk because it narrows the bore of the blood vessel and provides a rough surface for the clot to stick to. This condition can also affect other parts of circulation and is probably the main cause of stroke in elderly people. We should all try to reduce the risk of developing atherosclerosis, though clearly the younger you are, the more effective prevention is likely to be.

The development of atherosclerosis is strongly linked with high levels of cholesterol, a type of fat, in the blood. Populations with low blood cholesterol levels have less atherosclerosis than those with high levels, and people with very high levels can develop atherosclerosis early and die from a heart attack even before the age of thirty. The level of cholesterol in the blood is affected by genetic and environmental factors. It is the amount of fat eaten that influences blood cholesterol rather than cholesterol in the food. Eggs are particularly high in cholesterol and some people have excluded them for this reason. Yet they have a minor effect compared with a high saturated fat intake. Saturated fats, such as butter and coconut oil, increase blood cholesterol levels and the tendency of the blood to clot, while polyunsaturated fats, such as sunflower seed and corn oil (see pages 15–17) have a weaker but opposite effect.

In the average Western diet, including the lactovegetarian diet, most saturated fat comes from dairy products. Vegan diets contain relatively small amounts of saturated fats and no cholesterol, but plenty of polyunsaturated fats. Blood cholesterol levels are much lower in vegans than either meat eaters or lactovegetarians and are similar to the levels in populations where atherosclerosis is rare. The blood of both vegans and vegetarians clots less readily than meat eaters'. Vegans should be less prone to both atherosclerosis and coronary heart disease than meat eaters or ovo-lactovegetarians. This view is supported by studies on Seventh Day Adventists, which show that the male vegan members have a lower incidence of heart disease than vegetarian or meat-eating members.

Fiber

One very positive aspect of vegetarian and vegan diets is that they provide plenty of fiber, mainly from cereals, legumes and nuts, but also from fruit and vegetables. Dietary fiber is the structural material, sugars and gums from plants, that cannot be digested. It is not a nutrient but provides bulk in the diet. Because of its water-retaining properties, it helps food pass through the intestine faster, having a laxative effect. A high fiber intake may offer protection against several diseases of the large bowel and certainly prevents constipation. The richest sources of dietary fiber are bran, peas, beans and whole grain cereals. Certain types of fiber found in oats and legumes (beans, peas and lentils) seem to help control diabetes by slowing down the absorption of sugar into the blood. Most of the more up-to-date diabetic cookbooks include many recipes containing legumes.

One of the side effects of diets high in fiber is flatulence. It has been said that, "Vegetarianism is harmless enough, but apt to fill a man with self-righteousness and wind!" Flatulence is caused by bacteria living in the large bowel producing gases. The amount of gas produced is in proportion to the amount of carbohydrate reaching the bacteria. A diet high in fiber provides plenty of carbohydrates. Beans are particularly noted for their effects. They contain two sugars, stacchyose and raffinose, that cannot be digested and so combine with the bacteria in the intestine to form gas. Jerusalem artichokes contain a polysaccharide called inulin which cannot be digested, and onions and green pepper also contain fermentable carbohydrates, as well as sulfur-containing compounds responsible for the offensive smell of the emission.

Salt

It is known that high blood pressure is rare in communities with low salt intakes, while in communities with high intakes, this condition is common. High blood pressure is dangerous because it can lead to a blood vessel rupturing in the brain, causing a stroke. Studies of vegetarians show that they tend to consume less salt than meat eaters and some, but not all, studies have found that they have lower blood pressures. The cooking hints, see page 28, give advice on cutting down salt in your diet.

IS A VEGETARIAN DIET NUTRITIONALLY SOUND?

There are good and bad vegetarian diets. Fortunately there are fewer bad diets than good ones. Selecting a good diet is simple as long as you avoid the known pitfalls.

The particular questions people turning to vegetarianism ask are: which nutrients are normally provided by food of animal origin; and how can these be replaced by plant food? Food not only provides us with the nutrients we need, but as we have mentioned, may also play an important part in causing degenerative diseases such as coronary heart disease, stroke and large bowel cancer. It is thought that these may result from lifetime exposure to a diet high in fat, salt and sugar and low in fiber. So vegetarians should plan their eating with two objectives in mind: to ensure a good intake of the necessary nutrients, and to minimize this health risk.

The food we eat contains nutrients in different proportions, so the greater the number of good foods in your diet, the greater the variety of nutrients. People who eat only a few foods run the risk of their diet being inadequate. However, even a few foods can make up a sound diet if they are carefully chosen. Vegetarian and vegan diets can easily provide all the nutrients required if the foods are sensibly selected. Fruitarian diets are likely to be nutritionally inadequate and are not recommended (see page 10). Different components need to be considered in building up the right balance.

Energy

Food provides energy for muscular work and for body maintenance. It also contributes to body growth and repair of tissues. Requirements for energy are easily met by vegetarian and vegan diets as long as you eat enough. Calories, or to be more precise kilocalories, are the units used to measure the energy value of food. Calories can be provided by protein, fat, carbohydrates and alcohol. Fruits and vegetables tend to be bulky and provide few calories, so that a diet composed mainly of these foods will be low in calories. This may be desirable if you are an adult trying to lose weight, but can be disastrous for a young child who needs plenty of calories. Grains and dairy products, on the other hand, are high in calories and provide the nutrients for growth (the relative nutritional values of some high energy foods are shown in the table on page 16). When planning a vegetarian diet for young children, take care not to give a lot of food that is too bulky and make sure enough of the high energy foods are eaten (see opposite).

Protein

In the past, a great deal of unnecessary fuss was made about the amount and type of protein in the diet. Only small amounts are needed to provide material for the growth and repair of tissues. Since it cannot be stored in the body, a regular intake is needed (see also the table on page 23).

Vegetarians often worry that they are not getting enough protein of the right type. Yet vegetarian and vegan diets almost always provide sufficient amounts. The intake of protein is likely to be inadequate only when sago or cassava are the staple food, but neither of these usually forms a major part of Western vegetarian diets.

Different types of protein

1. High quality protein from milk, soybeans and eggs is efficiently used by the body and these are convenient sources of protein for the very young, the elderly and the sick. There are now many soybean products available, such as tofu (bean curd), soy milk and textured vegetable protein. Soy flour can also be used to thicken sauces and in baking.
2. Cereals (wheat, rice, rye, corn, millet, sorghum) and potatoes are most important sources. They contain about 10 per cent of their energy as protein, 10 per cent fat and 80 per cent carbohydrate; they are also rich in fiber. A diet based on these staple foods will ensure an adequate protein intake.
3. Nuts and legumes are rich in protein and when combined with cereals provide high quality protein.

When digested, proteins are broken down into amino acids which are then absorbed – what the body uses are these amino acids rather than protein. Eaten alone, plant proteins, with the notable exception of soybeans, are not used by the body as efficiently as eggs and milk because they have different amino acid patterns. However, if plant proteins from different sources are eaten together they complement each other and provide high

Protein source	Protein quality*
Egg	100
Human milk	100
Fish	90
Meat	80
Milk	80
Cereal and a legume (e.g., baked beans on toast)	80
Soybeans	75
Potato	70
Oatmeal	65
Sesame seeds	65
Cashew nuts	58
Rice (brown or white)	57
Sunflower seeds	56
Peas	48
Lentils	45
Red kidney beans	44
Whole-wheat bread	40

*Protein score – maximum 100 based on quality of whole eggs

Protein quality of some animal and plant foods

quality protein (for example baked beans on toast – see also the table above). Even if the plant proteins are eaten at different meals the complementary effect still works.

Fats
Small amounts of fat are needed to provide polyunsaturated fats and to allow the fat soluble vitamins such as A and D to be absorbed. Fat also makes food more palatable. Vegetarian and vegan diets often contain much more fat than is necessary for this reason. Most people prefer butter or margarine on their bread to bread alone. However, adding even small amounts of fat can double the calorie value. A slice of bread provides about 65 kcals whereas a slice of bread with 1 tablespoon of butter has about 160 kcals. It is very easy to consume too many calories with a high fat diet.

A high intake of fat is desirable for very young children as it provides both a concentrated supply of calories and helps in the absorption of fat soluble vitamins; the natural diet of the human baby, breast milk, is rich in fat. Diets high in fat are not so good for adults both because they are fattening and they may increase the risk of coronary heart disease in later life (see page 11). It is believed that many heart attacks could be prevented or deferred by reducing the intake of fat, particularly saturated fat. It is recommended that 30 per cent (around 70 g) of the daily energy intake should be from fat and not more than one-third of that should be from saturated fat. The recipes in this book broadly conform to that recommendation. Where the proportion of fat in any recipe is slightly higher, you should balance it out with accompanying low-fat foods such as bread, rice or potatoes.

	Weight (g)	Portion size	Protein (g)	Fat (g)	Dietary fiber (g)
Cereals					
Cookies, sugar	(20)	1	1.2	3.4	0.3
Bread					
White, enriched	(23)	1 slice	2.0	0.7	0.7
Wholewheat	(23)	1 slice	2.4	0.7	2.4
Fruitcake	(40)	1 piece	1.9	6.1	1.1
Rolled oats, cooked	(236)	1 cup	5.4	2.8	2.2
Rice					
Brown, cooked	(75)	½ cup	1.9	0.45	1.0
White, cooked	(75)	½ cup	1.5	0.1	0.5
Nuts, shelled					
Almonds, dried (unblanched)	(15)	12 to 15 nuts	2.8	8.1	2.4
Brazil	(15)	4 med nuts	2.2	9.9	1.5
Filberts	(15)	10 to 12 nuts	1.6	9.5	1.3
Walnuts, English	(15)	8 to 15 halves	2.3	9.7	1.1
Peanuts, roasted, w/skin	(15)	1 Tablespoon	4.0	7.0	1.3
Legumes					
Red kidney beans, cooked	(100)	⅔ cup	7.8	0.5	8.8
Lentils, cooked, drained	(100)	⅔ cup	7.8	tr	3.8
Soybeans					
Bean curd	(100)	3½ oz.	7.8	4.2	0.3
Milk	(263)	1 cup	8.9	3.9	0.0
Dairy					
Cheeses					
American, past, proc	(28)	1 oz.	6.5	8.4	0.0
Cottage Cheese, low fat 1%	(225)	1 cup	28	2.3	0.0
Eggs	(48)	1 med	6.2	5.5	0.0
Milk					
Skim	(246)	1 cup	8.0	0.4	0.0
Whole	(244)	1 cup	8.5	8.6	0.0
Miscellaneous					
Fats, Oils	(14)	1 Tablespoon	0.0	14.0	0.0
Butter	(15)	1 Tablespoon	0.1	12.2	0.0
Margarine	(15)	1 Tablespoon	0.1	12.2	0.0
Potatoes, boiled in skin	(100)	1 medium	2.1	0.5	2.1
Sugar, white granular	(12)	1 tablespoon	0.0	0.0	0.0

Protein, fat and dietary fiber in portions of food

All fats consist of a mixture of different fatty acids. There are three types:

- Saturated
- Monounsaturated
- Polyunsaturated

Fats are categorized according to which fatty acid is predominant. Butter, coconut and palm oils are saturated fats. Olive and peanut oils are monounsaturated. Corn, safflower, sunflower and soybean oils are polyunsaturated. Margarine is made from a mixture of animal and vegetable fats but some brands contain vegetable oils only and are labelled accordingly. The blend of oils used in margarine manufacture varies from day to day depending on the market price of the oils. Palm oil is the main vegetable oil used along with soybean, rapeseed and sunflower seed oils. Hard margarines (including the vegan variety) are saturated fats just like butter, but so are many of the soft tub margarines, except for those that claim to be high in polyunsaturates. Low-fat spreads differ from margarine, containing 40–60 per cent fat compared with the 80 per cent in margarine. The balance is made up by water.

Nuts and cheese, except cottage cheese and low-fat cheeses, have large amounts of fat but are also rich in protein.

The amount of fat supplied by any food depends not only on the amount you consume but also the fat content of the food. For example, whole milk contains only 3.5 per cent fat but because a lot is drunk it contributes a large amount of fat to most people's diet.

It is difficult to know how much fat is in a food just by looking at it. Cakes, pastries and cookies may contain large amounts added during their preparation. The way food is cooked will also affect the fat content; frying especially leads to an increased amount (see also Cooking Hints).

Carbohydrates

The cultivated seeds, fruits and roots that contain concentrated supplies of carbohydrates provide the basis of vegetarian diets. Carbohydrates exist in two forms, as starches and as sugars. As a rule, fruits are a source of sugar and seeds and roots a source of starches. Digestion breaks the starches down into sugars which are then absorbed.

Starchy carbohydrate foods, such as bread, pasta, rice and potatoes are considered a healthier source of calories than fat or alcohol; they also contain other nutrients in useful amounts. Sugar or sucrose, which is derived from sugar beet or sugar cane, is highly purified and provides no other nutrients. For this reason it has been called a source of empty calories. As well as being a quick way to get fat, eating large amounts of refined sugar leads to tooth decay. Sugar is fermented by bacteria in the mouth and produces acids which can dissolve the enamel of the teeth. There is no need to cut out jam or sugar in cooking entirely or to worry about the small amounts of sugar in prepared foods like baked beans. It is the sugar consumed between meals as candies, cookies, cakes and soft drinks that seems to be most harmful. Contrary to the widely held belief, brown sugar, molasses and honey differ very little from refined white sugar nutritionally and so should be used in moderation.

Minerals

A number of minerals are needed in small amounts and can be found in many foods. Some that are essential for health in small amounts are harmful in excess, for example sodium and fluoride. Vegetarians should make sure that they get enough calcium and iron and that they limit their intake of sodium.

Calcium is needed to harden bones and teeth. When the body supply is inadequate, bone formation is affected leading to stunted growth in children and bone deformities (called rickets), and osteomalacia (softening of the bones) in adults. These disorders are nearly always caused by vitamin D deficiency and very rarely by an inadequate calcium intake.

Lactovegetarians are likely to get enough in milk and its products but vegans' calcium intakes may be low. Most cereals and staple foods contain very little. Drinking water, especially in hard water areas, may provide some and sesame seeds are another good source. The table below lists other foods with a good supply of calcium. By eating these freely, an adequate amount of calcium should be available to vegans.

The absorption of calcium is regulated by the amount of vitamin D in your diet, but it is also affected by other plant foods. Many plants, for example rhubarb and spinach, contain compounds called oxalates which react with calcium to form calcium oxalate and this cannot be absorbed by the body. Wheat flour and oats contain phytic acid which interferes with the absorption of several minerals including calcium, iron and zinc. Phytic acid is broken down by yeast, so that when wheat flour is made into bread and leavened with yeast, the phytic acid is destroyed (see also Cooking Hints).

White bread has less phytic acid which interferes with calcium absorption. At the end of World War II a study was carried out on children in a German orphanage to see if a diet providing plenty of bread, made from white, brown or whole-wheat flours, but minimal amounts of milk, would support normal growth. Whatever the type of bread they ate, all the children had a high rate of growth even though some had previously been malnourished. So if plenty of vegetables and wheat of any type are eaten, your calcium intake will be satisfactory.

Almonds	6 tablespoons	Milk	
Baking powder	½ teaspoon	cows'	3½ fl. oz.
Brazil nuts	15	human	1½ cups
Broccoli	¼ lb.	Molasses, blackstrap	1 tablespoon
Cheese		Sesame seeds	4 teaspoons
Cheddar	1-inch cube	Soy flour	½ cup
cottage, low-fat	1 cup	Spinach, cooked	¾ cup
Parmesan, grated	scant 2 tablespoons	Turnip greens, cooked	¼ cup
Figs, dried	⅓ cup	White bread, enriched	6 slices
Hard water	1 quart	Whole-wheat bread	5 slices
Navy beans	⅓ cup	Yogurt, plain	⅓ cup

Portions of some foods providing 125 mg calcium

Almonds	⅔ cup	Navy beans, dry	¼ cup
Barley, pearl	1 cup	Pumpkin seeds	¼ cup
Cashew nuts	¾ cup	Rolled oats, dry	1 cup
Curry powder	1 teaspoon	Sesame seeds	¼ cup
Dark green leafy		Soybeans, dry	¼ cup
vegetables, cooked	1 cup	Sunflower seeds	6 tablespoons
Lentils, dry	⅓ cup	Walnuts, black	½ cup
Lima beans, cooked	1 cup	Wheatgerm	⅔ cup
Millet	⅓ cup	Whole-wheat bread	8 slices

Portions of some plant foods providing 4 mg iron

Iron   A large proportion of the iron in meat eaters' diets comes from meat, especially liver, and many vegetarians worry about becoming anemic when they first give up meat. Yet this rarely happens, probably because there are plenty of vegetable sources of iron (see table above).

Iron is needed in small amounts to form hemoglobin, the red oxygen carrying pigment in the blood. Iron deficiency results in anemia (low levels of hemoglobin), causing tiredness, weakness and giddiness. From our studies there is no evidence of an increase in the incidence of anemia among white vegetarians and vegans compared with the rest of the population, and they have also been found to have higher iron intakes, derived mainly from leafy vegetables and unrefined cereals, especially whole-wheat bread. On the other hand, anemia seems to be more common in Asian vegetarians living in Western societies. This may be because their staple food, white rice, contains less iron than whole-wheat bread.

How can you insure a good supply of iron in a vegetarian diet?
Although iron from plant foods is not so well absorbed as iron of animal origin, it is much improved by being combined with vitamin C, which occurs in many fruits and vegetables. Again, the importance of varying your diet is obvious. Whole-wheat bread, legumes, nuts and dark green leafy vegetables are better sources of iron than fruit and starchy foods such as potatoes. Occasionally using a cast iron cooking pan can also slightly boost your iron intake without being harmful.

Vitamins
Vitamins are needed for health in very small amounts because our bodies are not able to manufacture enough of them from other dietary sources. Various disorders such as night blindness, scurvy and rickets have been identified for centuries but were found only in this century to be associated with a lack of a specific vitamin. Although there are many vitamins, the number of deficiencies that occur naturally is limited.

As the vitamins were discovered, each was first labelled with a letter of the alphabet. Once a vitamin had been isolated and its chemical structure characterized, it was given a name. For example, vitamin A is called retinol. The alphabetic system is still useful because some vitamins appear as a group of different compounds. Vitamin B_{12} exists in several forms:

cyanocobalamin, sulphitocobalamin and hydroxycobalamin. It is also useful to refer to the B-complex vitamins (thiamin, riboflavin, niacin, biotin, pyridoxine, folate) as a group because they tend to be found together in the same types of foods such as yeast extracts and whole grain cereals.

Vitamins are either fat soluble – A, D, E and K – or water soluble – the B vitamins and vitamin C. The fat soluble vitamins can be stored in the body and this means that a regular intake is not essential. It may take several years to deplete the body stores of these. The water soluble vitamins can be stored for a comparatively short period, but even then it takes several weeks for a deficiency to develop.

Are vegetarians in danger of vitamin deficiency?   All the vitamins can be provided by foods of plant origin, but vitamins D and B_{12} are sometimes lacking in vegan and vegetarian diets.

Fruits and vegetables provide vitamins A, C, E and K, and cereals, grains and nuts the B-complex and vitamin E; so fruit and vegetables complement cereals, grains and nuts to provide a good balance. Vitamin A deficiency is only common among non-meat eaters in parts of the world where people eat very few colored fruits and vegetables. You could produce a B-complex deficiency by making a refined cereal staple such as white rice too high a proportion of your diet, but this would be easily averted by eating whole grain cereals or foods rich in the vitamins, such as yeast extract. Refining cereals means that the outer part of the grain which contains most of the B-complex vitamins and fiber is removed. Some vitamins are added back to white flour by bakers when they make white bread. However, whole-wheat bread is still nutritionally better than white bread because of its fiber content.

Vitamin D is usually obtained through exposing the skin to sunlight. When sunshine is limited, particularly during the winter months, the amount stored may be insufficient and so extra vitamin D has to be provided in the diet. It is necessary for the absorption of calcium, and vitamin D deficiency causes rickets and osteomalacia (see page 18). The elderly who tend not to go into the sun and young children with high rates of bone growth are vulnerable.

Vitamin D is found in very few foods naturally, mainly fish and liver. However, a synthetic form is added to margarine and milk. The amount provided by eating margarine is likely to be considerably lower than the recommended amount and so it is probably wise to give vitamin D supplements to vegans, especially during the winter months.

Vitamin B_{12} is the one vitamin most likely to be deficient in vegan and vegetarian diets. It is made exclusively by microorganisms: cereals, fruits, nuts, legumes, vegetables and other plant foods do not contain it unless contaminated by microorganisms that produce it, or by insects. Animals cannot make vitamin B_{12} and depend on microorganisms for it. It is stored in the liver and kidney and so is found in high concentrations in these foods. It is also found in all flesh and dairy foods. Some fermented foods

Beer, draft	2½ cups
Cheese	
Cheddar	¾ cup grated
cottage	½ cup
Egg	1 large
Milk	
cows'	1 cup
soy	¼ cup
Yeast extract	½ teaspoon

Portions of some foods providing one microgram of vitamin B_{12}

contain B_{12}, for example beer and pressed bean curd, but unlike the other B-complex vitamins it is not in whole grain cereal and yeast extract.

The possible effects of B_{12} deficiency are a type of anemia, monthly periods stopping (amenorrhea) and a nervous disorder causing a tingling sensation in the fingers and toes, leading to paralysis. The anemia can be prevented and cured by another vitamin, folic acid. Since vegans and vegetarians tend to have high intakes of folic acid, because they eat plenty of green vegetables, nuts and refined cereals, they rarely have the anemia associated with vitamin B_{12} deficiency. Consequently, the nervous symptoms, first the tingling and then a loss of sense of touch, are usually the first signs. The deficiency can be remedied with a vitamin B_{12} supplement. If untreated, it will progress to cause permanent paralysis and can be fatal. Vitamin B_{12} deficiency can be discovered only by a properly qualified medical practitioner after laboratory tests, so you should talk to your doctor if you think there is any danger of this lack in your diet.

The requirement is very small, about one microgram daily and even unsupplemented vegan diets will contain about half a microgram. Vegetarians who eat eggs and milk regularly are likely to have sufficient intakes but vegans may be at risk.

You should have a fairly regular intake (at least three times a week) as you cannot absorb more than about five micrograms in food or pill form at a time. We recommend that lactovegetarians who have only small amounts of milk products (less than 1¼ cups milk or ¾ cup grated cheese daily), as well as all vegans, eat foods supplemented with vitamin B_{12} or take supplements.

The vitamin is produced commercially by growing bacteria on vegetable growth media. This is used to supplement a number of vegan foods, particularly yeast extracts and soybean milk. The blue-green algae Spirulina, sold in health food shops, is a very rich source and is acceptable to many vegans although it is not very palatable. Very recently vitamin B_{12} has been added to some breakfast cereals. You can check this by reading the labels on the packages. The amounts of foods providing one microgram of vitamin B_{12} are shown in the table above. The need for vegans to insure that they have an adequate supply of vitamin B_{12} in their diet cannot be overemphasized.

Are other vitamin supplements necessary?   There should be no need for vegans and vegetarians to take any vitamin supplements other than D and B_{12} (except during pregnancy, see page 24). However, many people do choose to take them as an insurance policy. While there is no harm in doing this, there has not yet been any proof that they bring benefits. Because small amounts of vitamins are necessary, it does not follow that larger amounts will be better.

Manufactured vitamin preparations should be regarded as medicines and the stated dose should not be exceeded; they should also be kept out of the reach of young children. An excess of water soluble vitamins is generally not a problem because it can be passed in the urine. But very high doses of many of these vitamins produce drug-like effects, for example the B vitamin nicotinic acid in large amounts (greater than 80 mg) will lead to flushing which lasts for about two hours, and too much vitamin B_6 can cause neurological disorders. Excessive intakes of fat soluble vitamins can be more dangerous because they cannot be passed easily in the urine and so accumulate in the body. Too much carrot juice or ß-carotene, which is the provitamin A, makes the skin turn orange. Large amounts of Vitamin A (retinol) cause sickness, headaches and the skin to peel. Deaths have been reported in extreme cases. Vitamin D when taken in excess can cause bone deformities.

HOW MUCH FOOD DO I NEED?

It is impossible to say accurately how much food any one person needs because everybody's requirements and energy expenditure are different. Therefore, it is only useful to give guidelines on the relative proportions of food in the diet (see the table opposite).

There is no need to plan all the nutrients in the correct proportions. No one eats the same food at each meal day in, day out and any deficit in one meal should be made up in another. What is important is to make potatoes or a cereal such as bread or rice the basis of your meals, with fruit and vegetables providing complementary nutrients. Generally whole grain cereals are nutritionally superior to refined cereals, but white bread and white rice are still good foods. The greater the variety in your diet the more you avoid any risk of deficiency. At the same, time your food is much more enjoyable. Remember the following points when deciding what foods to provide:

- In the past many vegetarians compensated by eating more dairy products and eggs when they gave up meat and fish. As the current view is that it is probably healthier to limit the amount of fat, particularly the saturated fat in your diet, it makes sense to be less dependent on milk and cheese and to use plant alternatives.
- You should make sure when cutting down on dairy fat that you maintain your intake of vitamin A. This is easily done by eating a salad containing leafy vegetables with your meals every day and by eating carrots regularly.
- For the other vitamins, aim to eat at least one piece of fresh fruit

	Men (23–50 yrs)	Women (23–50 yrs)
Energy (kcal)	2700	2000
Protein (grams)	56	44
Carbohydrates (grams)	320–380	290–340
Minimum carbohydrate intake for person on weight reducing diet	100	100
Fats (grams)	40–80	36–72
Ideal dietary fiber intake (grams)	30	30
Calcium (grams)	800	800
Iron (mg)	10	18

Recommended daily amounts of nutrients for adult men and women

a day. Oranges and other citrus fruits are particularly rich in vitamin C.

- Whole-wheat bread, preferably not spread with butter or margarine, is an excellent accompaniment to soups, vegetable stews and pasta dishes and is particularly nourishing. It is a good idea always to have a generous supply of bread available at any meal.
- A moderate amount of alcohol, one can of beer a day or a couple of glasses of wine, seems to do no harm and helps many people to relax.

As a rough guide this meal plan, based on our studies of adult vegetarian diets, is very typical and can be recommended:

Breakfast granola with milk or soy milk
toast with margarine or butter and marmalade
fresh orange juice
unsweetened tea, coffee or herb tea
Break coffee, fruit and plain cookie
Lunch green salad
whole-wheat bread and peanut butter
or baked potato with filling, e.g., cottage cheese
fruit
Supper cooked meal with salad/fresh vegetables
fruit

Weight watching on a vegetarian diet
Ideally your body weight should remain the same throughout adult life. However, most people put on weight as they grow older. Increased weight beginning in middle age is due to an excessive intake of calories for the amount used. You can easily see if you are overweight by standing in front of a mirror without any clothes on. If you can pinch more than one inch of fat around your waist you are overweight and that may increase the risk

of your getting diseases such as heart disease, diabetes or arthritis.

The only proven way of losing weight is to eat fewer calories. This is most easily done by restricting alcohol, fatty foods such as cheese and nuts, and sugary foods such as cakes and cookies. You can eat as much fruit and vegetables as you like – these provide few calories but a lot of bulk. Cut down on starchy foods such as bread and potatoes as they are fattening in excess, but do not cut them out. Not only are they an important source of protein and vitamins for vegetarians but including a moderate amount of carbohydrate in a reducing diet is both safer and more effective.

Try to eat several small meals a day rather than a few large ones and aim to lose weight gradually, at a rate of about two pounds weekly. Once you have achieved your ideal body weight, adjust your food intake so that you neither gain nor lose weight. Weigh yourself regularly, and as soon as you start to put on weight again cut back on what you eat. The recipes in this book give calorie values so you can plan a controlled diet around them.

PREGNANCY AND LACTATION

Both pregnancy and lactation proceed quite normally in vegetarian mothers. Pregnancy increases the body's need for nutrients but the body uses them more efficiently so that dietary requirements hardly change. Iron losses are reduced by your periods stopping and iron is better absorbed from the food you eat. Protein is used more efficiently and energy is conserved as fat. The idea that a mother should eat for two is wrong. There is no reason for a woman who is already eating a good diet to change it when she becomes pregnant. Indeed, a woman should be eating a good diet before she even considers becoming pregnant.

There may, however, be a danger of vitamin deficiency around the time of conception. Vitamin B_{12} and folic acid are essential for cell division and a deficiency of these vitamins is suspected as being the cause of spina bifida. A recent study of high-risk mothers found that among those who took multivitamin supplements around conception and during the first few weeks of pregnancy, there were fewer spina bifida babies than among those who did not.

The fetus gets its supply of oxygen from the maternal blood and anemia will retard its growth. So many doctors prescribe iron and folic acid tablets to mothers (vegetarian and meat eaters) during pregnancy as a safeguard against anemia. Supplementing your diet with iron during pregnancy also means that your baby will be born with a greater supply of iron.

During pregnancy, women lay down a considerable amount of body fat, usually about 9 lbs. This is an entirely natural process and happens to all mammals. The fat acts as an energy supply to help subsidize lactation. Each kilogram of fat deposited during pregnancy can be cashed in during lactation to yield 9000 calories, which is sufficient to support the cost in energy of producing 11 quarts of milk. Mothers who put on a lot of fat while they are pregnant do not need to eat as much during lactation as those who put on very little. Two pieces of advice if you are pregnant or breastfeeding: do not attempt to diet; if you feel ravenously hungry, eat more.

The amount of breast milk you produce is affected by your diet to some extent, but also by your hormones and psychological factors. If you do not produce enough milk, it is generally due to these factors rather than an inadequate diet. The vitamin content of your breast milk, though, is definitely affected by your diet. If you have a vitamin deficiency, it can only mean your baby will too. A few years ago a very severe case of vitamin B_{12} deficiency was discovered in a baby breast fed by a vegan mother who had not been taking vitamin B_{12} supplements. The deficiency in the baby was treated by giving his mother B_{12} supplements. We have measured the levels of vitamins in the breast milk of vegans and vegetarians and have found low levels of vitamin B_{12} in the milk from those mothers who did not take supplements or eat foods containing the vitamins. Women who either took supplements or ate food supplemented with vitamin B_{12} had levels in their breast milk similar to meat eaters.

Vegan and vegetarian mothers must make sure they have a source of vitamin B_{12} in their diet; but we have usually found higher levels of the other vitamins in the breast milk of vegetarians and vegans than in the milk of meat eaters.

Feeding the vegetarian baby

Most vegetarians and vegans breast feed their babies well into the second year and then wean them onto their respective diets. These children's growth and development are normal, but there is a tendency for them, especially the vegans, to be shorter and lighter than average. Although no baby should be grossly underweight under the age of five years, there is no evidence that being smaller than average is harmful; it may even be an advantage. A gradual slow growth rate is more likely to prolong life.

Breast milk is the best food for the human baby, providing all the nutrients necessary for at least the first six months and, under optimal conditions, up to a year. The supply begins soon after the baby is born. The more quickly the baby is put to the breast after birth, the more likely lactation is to be successful; and the more a breast is suckled, the more milk it will supply. So demand feeding is best. The amount of milk babies take varies greatly. Some babies thrive on two and one-half cups and others need one quart to maintain the same rate of growth. Usually babies take between two and one-half to three cups per day in the first three months. The best way of knowing whether your baby is getting enough milk is to check the weight gain. Most babies gain four to five ounces a week in the first three months and by the age of six months they should have doubled their birth weight.

If your supply of breast milk is inadequate, formulas based on a modified cows' milk can be used. There are special soybean formulas developed for feeding babies who cannot tolerate cows' milk. These soy milks should be used only as complementary feedings for babies under six months. Never use them as the sole source of food for any length of time without consulting your doctor. After six months, once your baby has started taking other food, you can use soy milks freely.

Weaning foods such as puréed fruit and vegetables and baby cereals and breads can be introduced at six months. The aim is to get your baby used to the idea of accepting food other than milk. When you begin to give more solid food, whole-wheat bread, spread with margarine and smooth peanut butter or a yeast extract, is good to start with. Do not fill your baby up with bulky and watery foods like puréed green vegetables and fruit – these are not sufficiently concentrated forms of nutrition. Make sure that the food is smooth and does not contain bits that could lead to choking; never give unground nuts to young children.

Beyond the age of one, your baby should be introduced to the food the rest of the family eats. Make sure that the meals provide a mixture of a legume and a cereal for high quality protein, for example baked beans on toast or rice and lentils. Additional milk will not be necessary if your baby is breast fed, but some types of whole milk (and this can be soy milk) is needed in the human diet up until the age of two. Do not use skim milk to feed your child under the age of one year.

Children brought up as vegans need vitamin D drops from the age of six months, but do not exceed the stated dose. As long as your baby is breast fed, vitamin B_{12} supplements are not necessary if your intake is adequate. Nevertheless, it is a good idea to use foods containing B_{12} such as soy milk and yeast extracts, during weaning.

After five

From now on there is no need for special food. The balanced vegetarian diet you eat yourself will also supply what is necessary for your child's growth and development. The quantities children eat vary from one to another by as much as several hundred calories per day. As long as your child is growing steadily without becoming overweight, you should not be unduly worried about calorie intake.

Vegetarian parents have to remember that as children get older you are less able to regulate what they eat. Eating is an important part of social life besides providing nutrients. Vegetarian children will often eat what they like in other children's houses. It is probably more important to allow them to mix socially than to insist on their adhering strictly to vegetarian principles.

The recommendations in this book are for a balanced diet that will sustain a hungry teenager as well as a fully grown adult. The quantities needed will be in line with what you'd expect to give any adolescent – up to twice as much as you might eat yourself. It would be encouraging for a lone vegetarian in the household to cook the recipes in this book sometimes for the whole family.

COOKING HINTS

Here are the ways to get the best nutrition from your vegetarian diet, as well as achieve better textures and flavors in the foods.

Retaining the vitamins
Food preparation can greatly affect the vitamin content:

- Boiling causes some of the water soluble vitamins to be leached out in the cooking water, and if the cooking water is thrown away, vitamins will be lost.
- Prolonged cooking and exposure to air destroys riboflavin, folate, vitamin B_{12} and vitamin C.
- Some vitamin C is destroyed if food is chopped up and left for several hours exposed to air before it is eaten.
- Vitamins are lost when vegetables are cooked and then kept warm for several hours before being eaten.

The best way to conserve vitamins in vegetables is to chop them up immediately before use, cook them in a minimum amount of water and serve them as soon as they are cooked. Prepare salads as close to the time they are eaten as possible.

Preserving food can lead to vitamin losses. Most of the vitamin C is lost when fruit and vegetables are canned or bottled, although many manufacturers now put vitamin C back into the food. Freezing is usually the best preserving method with only minimal losses. It also retains fresher flavors.

Fats
To cut down on your intake of saturated fats:

- Use cottage cheese or low-fat cheese in place of cream cheese.
- Use skim, low-fat or soy milk in place of whole milk.
- Use low-fat plain yogurt in place of cream.
- Use olive, corn, safflower or sunflower oil in place of hard fats.
- Use either a low-fat spread or a margarine high in polyunsaturates instead of butter or ordinary margarine.
- Avoid rich cakes and cookies.

Frying   Using a Chinese wok greatly reduces the amount of fat in cooking. Its convex shape means only a little is needed for light frying.

Baking (vegan)   Recipes in this book using butter, such as tarts and pies, can be equally successfully cooked with one of the hard vegan margarines (kosher varieties). The nutritional analyses will be the same.

Salad dressings   Aim to use very little oil in dressings, and introduce the fresh flavors of herbs such as basil, mint and marjoram and lemon juice or flavored vinegars.

Bread Making

The longer you leave your bread to rise the more phytic acid in the bread will be broken down by the yeast. This will make the minerals in your diet more available (see page 18).

Legumes

Dried beans must never be eaten raw after soaking, unless sprouted, as they contain natural toxins. These poisonous substances are destroyed after boiling for ten minutes. For red kidney beans, rapid boiling for the first ten minutes is essential. For other types, the water must reach boiling point for at least ten minutes during the cooking. Do not use a crock pot for beans, since the water never reaches boiling point.

Peas, beans and lentils will cook more quickly if salt is not added during cooking. Most beans take one and one-half hours to cook in an open pan or thirty minutes in a pressure cooker. Lentils are best cooked in an open pan and take about twenty to thirty minutes to cook. Red or Egyptian lentils are the fastest cooking and don't need soaking.

Salt

Much of the salt we eat is added to our food at the table or during preparation and cooking. As there are no positive advantages to eating larger amounts than necessary, it is best to avoid adding salt during cooking. At the table, season a prepared dish as lightly as possible. Although the taste of food may first appear bland, you can soon adapt, and will find the flavor of freshly cooked vegetables much more subtle. The salt occurring naturally in foods such as cheese will give you enough for your body's needs.

Yeast extracts contain large amounts of salt but are extremely valuable to the vegetarian in other ways, providing B-complex vitamins. Because they are used in small amounts, they make only a small contribution to the total salt intake.

APPETIZERS

Perhaps the highest intake of unhealthy food the majority consumes comes from eating commercially made snacks – the most easily accessible junk food. It is not difficult to alter this trend completely by preparing enticing food which can be used for parties or enjoyed instead of a first course.

Beans are a great source of fiber and will pureé beautifully. Their bland earthy taste can be given zest with addition of spices, herbs and flavored oils and vinegars. Whole-wheat bread can be cut to make croutons. A variety of vegetables can be stuffed.

Croutons · V

1 loaf whole-wheat bread, cut in   2-inch (5 cm.) slices
6 garlic cloves
Olive oil

Preheat oven to 400F (205C).

Cut a circle in middle of each bread slice 1-inch (2.5-cm.) deep, leaving a ½-inch (1.5-cm.) rim. In a small skillet, sauté garlic in oil. Remove garlic; discard. Arrange croutons on a baking sheet. Brush lightly with garlic oil. Bake in preheated oven 10 minutes or until crisp and browned. Drain on paper towels. Fill center with any dip or spread on pages 30 to 32.

Per crouton: 90 kcal/2 g protein/5 g fat/10 g carbohydrate/negligible fiber

Garlic Toast · V

1 large loaf whole-wheat bread,   sliced
6 garlic cloves
Olive oil

Preheat oven to 400F (205C)

Cut each slice of bread in 4 squares. In a small skillet, sauté garlic in oil. Remove garlic; discard. Arrange bread on a baking sheet. Brush lightly with garlic oil. Bake in preheated oven 10 minutes or until crisp. Drain on paper towels. Use toast for any dip or spread on pages 30 to 32.

Per toast: 90 kcal/2 g protein/5 g fat/8 g carbohydrate/2 g fiber

Fresh Cheese Spread

⅔ cup cottage cheese or
   Neufchâtel cheese
1 bunch green onions, finely
   chopped

2 drops hot-pepper sauce
Salt
Pepper

If using cottage cheese, process in a blender until smooth. In a small bowl, mix cottage cheese or Neufchâtel cheese, onions and hot-pepper sauce. Season with salt and pepper. Refrigerate until chilled. Makes ⅔ cup.

Total recipe: 400 kcal/13 g protein/37 g fat/5 g carbohydrate/2 g fiber

Ricotta Spread

1 cup ricotta cheese
⅔ (3 oz.) pkg. Neufchâtel cheese
1 onion, thinly sliced, or 2 shallots,
   thinly sliced

2 teaspoons green peppercorns
Salt
Pepper

In a blender, process ricotta cheese until smooth. Add Neufchâtel cheese, onions and peppercorns. Season with salt and pepper. Process to a paste. Refrigerate until chilled. Makes 1½ cups.

Total recipe: 670 kcal/28 g protein/60 g fat/5 g carbohydrate/1 g fiber

Black Bean Dip   V

⅔ cup dried black beans
2 tablespoons walnut oil
⅓ cup grated fresh gingerroot
1 teaspoon cumin

1 teaspoon coriander
Salt
Pepper

In a small bowl, cover beans with water. Soak 8 to 10 hours. Drain. In a large saucepan, cover beans with clean water. Boil 10 minutes. Drain. In a medium saucepan, heat oil. Add ginger, cumin and coriander. Cook 1 to 2 minutes. Add beans and enough water to cover beans 2 inches. Bring to a boil. Reduce heat. Simmer 1½ hours or until beans are tender. Drain; reserve liquid.

In a blender, process beans and enough cooking liquid to obtain a smooth purée. Season with salt and pepper. Makes 2¼ cups.

Total recipe: 650 kcal/31 g protein/32 g fat/63 g carbohydrate/35 g fiber

Navy Bean Dip

⅔ cup dried navy beans
¼ cup olive oil
1 tablespoon fresh summer
 savory
Grated peel and juice of 1 lemon

2 bay leaves
2 tablespoons low-fat plain
 yogurt
Salt
Pepper

In a small bowl, cover beans with water. Soak 2 hours; drain. In a medium saucepan, heat oil. Add beans, summer savory and lemon peel and juice. Cook 1 to 2 minutes; stir. Add enough water to cover beans 2 inches. Add bay leaves. Bring to a boil. Reduce heat. Simmer 1½ hours or until beans are tender. Drain; retain cooking liquid. Remove bay leaves.

In a blender, process beans, yogurt and enough of cooking liquid to obtain a smooth purée. Season with salt and pepper. Makes 2¼ cups.

Total recipe: 870 kcal/32 g protein/55 g fat/66 g carbohydrate/36 g fiber

Hummus ⟦V⟧

¾ cup garbanzo beans
Peel and juice of 2 lemons
2 bay leaves
2 tablespoons olive oil
4 garlic cloves, minced

1½ cups fresh mint, finely
 chopped
Juice of 1 lemon
Salt
Pepper

In a small bowl, cover beans with water and soak for 8 to 10 hours. Drain. In a medium saucepan, combine peel and juice of 2 lemons, bay leaves and enough water to cover beans 2 inches. Bring to a boil. Reduce heat. Simmer 2 hours or until beans are tender. Drain; reserve cooking liquid. Discard peel and bay leaves.

In a blender, process beans, olive oil, garlic, mint, juice of 1 lemon and enough cooking liquid to obtain a smooth purée. Season with salt and pepper. Makes 2½ cups.

Total recipe: 1010 kcal/34 g protein/62 g fat/85 g carbohydrate/26 g fiber

Snow Pea Dip ⟦V⟧

1 lb. fresh snow peas
2 tablespoons butter or
 margarine

Salt
Pepper

Remove fibrous parts from snow peas. In a medium saucepan, cover snow peas with water. Cook until tender. In a blender, process snow peas and butter or margarine until smooth. Season with salt and pepper. Refrigerate until chilled. Makes 1½ cups.

Total recipe: 300 kcal/11 g protein/21 g fat/18 g carbohydrate/13 g fiber

Brussels Sprouts Dip $\boxed{V}$

1 lb. fresh Brussels sprouts	¼ teaspoon grated nutmeg
2 cups whole-wheat	2 drops hot-pepper sauce
breadcrumbs	Salt
Grated peel and juice of 1 lemon	Pepper
2 tablespoons walnut oil	

In a medium saucepan, cook Brussels sprouts in boiling salted water 5 minutes or until just tender. Drain. In a blender, process Brussels sprouts, breadcrumbs, lemon peel and juice, oil, nutmeg and hot-pepper sauce to a thick purée. Season with salt and pepper. Refrigerate until chilled. Makes 3 cups.

Total recipe: 780 kcal/26 g protein/54 g fat/51 g carbohydrate/23 g fiber

Cheese Bites   *Photograph, page 50*

¾ cup ricotta cheese	*To decorate:*
1 tablespoon Neufchâtel cheese	Pine nuts
½ teaspoon paprika	Pistachio nuts
½ teaspoon curry powder	Walnuts
½ teaspoon cumin	Dried fruit
½ teaspoon green peppercorns	
½ teaspoon cinnamon	
½ teaspoon turmeric	

In a blender, process ricotta cheese and Neufchâtel cheese until smooth. Divide mixture into 6 pieces. Roll into thimble shapes. Coat each piece with 1 spice. Decorate with nuts or fruit. Makes 6 pieces.

Total recipe: 455 kcal/14 g protein/44 g fat/1 g carbohydrate/negligible fiber

Gruyère Puffs

⅔ cup water
2 tablespoons butter or
   margarine
½ teaspoon salt

½ teaspoon cayenne pepper
¾ cup whole-wheat flour
4 eggs, beaten
1¾ cup shredded Gruyère cheese

Preheat oven to 400F (200C). Grease a baking sheet.

In a medium saucepan, bring water, butter or margarine, salt and cayenne pepper to a boil. Pour flour into water mixture in a steady stream, stirring continually until mixture leaves sides of pan. Remove from heat. Let cool. Slowly add eggs to cooled mixture, beating continuously. When dough absorbs eggs, mix in ¾ of cheese.

Drop tablespoons of dough on prepared baking sheet 2 inches (5 cm.) apart. Sprinkle remaining cheese over each puff. Bake in preheated oven 45 minutes or until golden brown. Serve hot. Makes 12 to 15 puffs.

Total recipe: 1245 kcal/60 g protein/80 g fat/76 g carbohydrate/11 g fiber

Falafel

1 cup dried garbanzo beans
1 teaspoon baking powder
2 large onions, finely chopped
6 garlic cloves, minced
1 teaspoon coriander
1 teaspoon cumin
1 teaspoon fennel seed

1 bunch fresh parsley, finely
   chopped
Salt
Pepper
2 egg whites, beaten stiff
2 tablespoons corn oil

In a large bowl, cover beans with water. Soak 8 to 10 hours. Drain. In a medium saucepan, add beans and enough water to cover beans 2 inches. Boil 2 hours or until tender. Drain. In a blender, process beans to a powder. In a medium bowl, mix beans, baking powder, onions, garlic, spices and parsley. Season with salt and pepper. Fold egg whites into mixture.

In a medium skillet, heat oil. Drop small spoonfuls of mixture into oil. Brown on all sides. Drain on paper towels. Serve warm. Makes approximately 20.

Total recipe: 1120 kcal/56 g protein/48 g fat/123 g carbohydrate/41 g fiber

Potato & Sesame Falafel

3 cups mashed potatoes
3 tablespoons sesame seed paste
2 tablespoons roasted sesame
  seeds

Salt
Pepper
2 egg whites, beaten stiff
2 tablespoons corn oil

In a medium bowl, mix potatoes, sesame seed paste and sesame seeds. Season with salt and pepper. Fold in egg whites. In a medium skillet, heat oil. Drop small spoonfuls of mixture into oil. Brown on all sides. Drain on paper towels. Serve warm. Makes 15 to 20.

Total recipe: 1590 kcal/30 g protein/109 g fat/138 g carbohydrate/10 g fiber

Potato Fingers

3 cups cooked mashed potatoes
1 cup shredded Cheddar cheese
⅔ cup whole-wheat flour
1 egg, beaten

Salt
Pepper
2 tablespoons corn oil

In a large bowl, mix potatoes, cheese, flour and egg. Season with salt and pepper. Cut in small pieces. Roll into small finger shapes. In a large skillet, heat corn oil. Brown Potato Fingers on all sides. Drain on paper towels. Serve warm. Makes 12 fingers.

Total recipe: 1685 kcal/47 g protein/95 g fat/171 g carbohydrate/13 g fiber

FIRST COURSES

The golden rule for eating well and healthfully is to have fresh and simple dishes. The best and most healthful first course is always fresh vegetables with or without a selection of dips. Any dip in this book can be served. Present fresh vegetables on a large center platter, or arrange a few on individual plates with a sauce.

Many tarts and quiches on page 62 and 71 can be served as first courses. Instead of one or two large tarts, prepare individual tartlets.

Avocado Sauce & Fresh Vegetables

Avocado Sauce:
2 large avocados, peeled, pitted
Grated peel and juice of 1 lemon
2 garlic cloves, minced
1 cup low-fat plain yogurt
Salt
Pepper

Fresh vegetables, cut in serving
  pieces

To garnish:
Fresh herbs

Avocado sauce
In a blender process avocado, lemon peel and juice, garlic and yogurt. Season with salt and pepper. Blend until smooth.

Arrange vegetables on individual plates. Pour a small amount of sauce on each plate. Garnish with fresh herbs. Makes 6 servings.

Total for Avocado Sauce: 1495 kcal/40 g protein/136 g fat/30 g carbohydrate/12 g fiber

Avocado with Onion & Green Peppercorn Sauce $\boxed{\text{V}}$

2 garlic cloves, minced
Grated peel and juice of 1 lemon
2 tablespoons olive oil
1 bunch green onions, chopped
Salt

Pepper
Crisp lettuce leaves
2 large avocados, peeled, halved,
  pitted
2 tablespoons green peppercorns

To make sauce, in a small bowl, mix garlic, lemon peel and juice, olive oil and onions. Season with salt and pepper. Arrange lettuce leaves on 4 individual plates. Slice each avocado half lengthwise several times, keeping pear shape. Place 1 avocado half on each plate. Pour sauce over avocado. Sprinkle peppercorns over each portion. Makes 4 servings.

Per serving: 410 kcal/7 g protein/41 g fat/4 g carbohydrate/4 g fiber

Pears with Guacamole $\boxed{V}$

2 avocados, peeled, pitted, sliced
1 small onion, chopped
2 garlic cloves, minced
Grated peel and juice of 1 lemon
2 tablespoons olive oil
1 fresh green chili, seeded,
   chopped
2 tomatoes, chopped

Salt
Pepper
4 pears, peeled, halved

To garnish:
Lettuce leaves
1 tablespoon cilantro, chopped

To make guacamole, in a blender process avocados, onion, garlic, lemon peel and juice, and olive oil to a purée. Add green chili and tomatoes to avocado mixture. Season with salt and pepper.

Spoon gaucamole in center of a large platter. Arrange pears around guacamole. Press pears lightly into guacamole. Garnish with lettuce leaves. Sprinkle cilantro over top. Makes 4 servings.

Per serving: 260 kcal/4 g protein/24 g fat/8 g carbohydrate/3 g fiber

Stuffed Artichokes   *Photograph, page 50*

4 large artichokes
⅔ cup low-fat plain yogurt
1 (14-oz.) can hearts of palm,
   drained, diced
Grated peel and juice of 1 lemon
2 garlic cloves, minced

1 large bunch fresh chives,
finely chopped
Salt
Pepper
1 tablespoon soy sauce

Cut off tops of pointed leaves of artichokes. In a large saucepan, boil artichokes in salted water 45 minutes or until tender. Drain well; cool. Remove center leaves from artichokes; leaving a wall of outside leaves. Reserve removed leaves. Cut out hairy chokes, leaving pad of flesh at bottom intact. Discard hairy chokes.

To make stuffing, using a sharp knife, scrape edible part from bottom of each reserved leaf. In a medium bowl, mix scraped artichoke flesh, yogurt, hearts of palm, lemon peel and juice, garlic and chives. Season with salt and pepper.

Spoon mixture into each prepared artichoke. Drizzle soy sauce over each stuffed artichoke. Makes 4 servings.

Per serving: 80 kcal/6 g protein/negligible fat/14 g carbohydrate/25 g fiber

Stuffed Zucchini

4 to 6 medium zucchini	Salt
1 medium onion, finely chopped	Pepper
1¼ cups cottage cheese	
1 tablespoon Dijon-style	*To garnish:*
mustard	Fresh parsley sprigs

Trim ends of zucchini. Slice in ½ lengthwise. Scoop out seeds in a boat-shaped indentation from each half. Invert on a paper towel. To make stuffing, in a small bowl, mix onion, cottage cheese and mustard. Season with salt and pepper. Spoon stuffing into zucchini. Press stuffing down firmly. Press sides of zucchini inwards around stuffing. Refrigerate 1 hour. Cut in ½-inch (1-cm.) slices. Arrange on a platter. Garnish with parsley. Makes 4 servings.

Per serving: 115 kcal/11 g protein/3 g fat/12 g carbohydrate/5 g fiber

Stuffed Peppers

1 bunch green onions, finely chopped	2 garlic cloves, minced
	Salt
1 large bunch fresh parsley, finely chopped	Pepper
	2 green bell peppers, tops removed, cored, seeded
½ cup crumbled Roquefort cheese	2 red bell peppers, tops removed, cored, seeded
1¼ cups cottage cheese	
2 tablespoons capers	

To make stuffing, in a medium bowl, mix onions, parsley, Roquefort cheese, cottage cheese, capers and garlic. Season with salt and pepper. Spoon stuffing into peppers. Push stuffing to bottom of peppers. Refrigerate 1 hour. Slice peppers crosswise in ½-inch (1-cm.) pieces. Arrange on a platter, alternating red and green peppers. Makes 4 servings.

Per serving: 320 kcal/11 g protein/29 g fat/5 g carbohydrate/3 g fiber

Stuffed Tomatoes

2 to 3 large beefsteak tomatoes, halved (allow ½ tomato per serving)
½ cup whole-wheat breadcrumbs
⅓ cup grated Parmesan cheese
1 tablespoon tomato purée

2 garlic cloves, minced
1 bunch fresh basil, finely chopped
Salt
Pepper
¼ cup shredded Gruyère cheese

Preheat oven to 400F (200C).

Scoop out seeds and juice from tomato halves. Reserve pulp. Leave exterior flesh intact. Set aside. To make stuffing, in a medium bowl, mix tomato pulp, breadcrumbs, Parmesan cheese, tomato purée, garlic and basil. Season with salt and pepper. Place tomato shells on a baking sheet. Spoon stuffing into tomato halves. Sprinkle Gruyère cheese over each tomato. Bake in preheated oven 10 minutes. Serve hot or cold. Makes 4 to 6 servings.

Per serving: 110 kcal/8 g protein/4 g fat/12 g carbohydrate/5 g fiber

Lettuce Rolls

12 large lettuce leaves
1 ripe avocado, peeled, pitted, chopped
1¼ cups cottage cheese
2 garlic cloves, minced
1 bunch green onions, finely chopped

3 tablespoons fresh mint, finely chopped
Salt
Pepper

In a large saucepan, blanch lettuce leaves in boiling water 1 to 2 minutes. Carefully drape leaves over a colander to drain. In a blender, process avocado, cottage cheese and garlic to a thick purée. In a medium bowl, mix purée, onions and mint. Season with salt and pepper.

Lay each lettuce leaf flat. Spoon 1 tablespoon of stuffing on end of each leaf. Roll up length of leaf, tucking in sides. Refrigerate 1 hour. Makes 12 rolls.

Per roll: 50 kcal/4 g protein/4 g fat/1 g carbohydrate/negligible fiber

Spinach Rolls

12 large fresh spinach leaves
1¼ cups cottage cheese
½ cup shredded Gruyère cheese
⅔ cup grated Parmesan cheese
2 garlic cloves, minced
1 tablespoon paprika

½ cup chopped walnuts
½ cup whole-wheat
 breadcrumbs
Salt
Pepper
Butter or margarine

Preheat oven to 350F (175C).

In a large saucepan, blanch spinach leaves in boiling water 1 to 2 minutes. Carefully drape leaves over a colander to drain. In a medium bowl, mix cottage cheese, Gruyère cheese and Parmesan cheese. Stir in garlic, paprika, walnuts and breadcrumbs. Season with salt and pepper.

Lay each spinach leaf flat. Spoon 1 tablespoon stuffing mixture on end of each leaf. Roll up length of leaf, tucking in sides. Arrange rolls in a shallow dish. Dot with butter or margarine. Cover with foil. Bake in preheated oven 20 minutes. Serve hot, warm or cold. Makes 12 rolls.

Per roll: 90 kcal/7 g protein/6 g fat/2 g carbohydrate/1 g fiber

Spinach Pâté   V

¼ cup butter or margarine
2 lbs. fresh leaf spinach,
 trimmed
Grated peel and juice of 1 lemon

⅛ teaspoon grated nutmeg
Salt
Pepper

In a large saucepan, melt butter or margarine. Add spinach leaves. Simmer, covered, 10 to 12 minutes or until spinach is reduced ⅔. Add lemon peel and juice and nutmeg. Season with salt and pepper. In a blender, process mixture until smooth. Pour into 4 individual ramekins. Refrigerate 1 hour or until set. Makes 4 servings.

Per serving: 170 kcal/12 g protein/13 g fat/2 g carbohydrate/10 g fiber

Spinach & Apricot Mousse   *Photograph, page 50*

¾ cup dried apricots
Water
1½ lbs. fresh spinach, trimmed
⅔ cup grated Parmesan cheese
½ cup shredded Gruyère cheese
⅔ cup low-fat plain yogurt

4 eggs
Salt
Pepper

To garnish:
Sprigs of parsley

In a small bowl, cover dried apricots with water. Soak 8 to 10 hours. In a small saucepan, cook apricots and liquid over low heat. Boil to reduce. Cool. Preheat oven to 400F (200C). Grease a 9″ × 5″ loaf pan. Line pan with waxed paper. Grease waxed paper.

In a large saucepan, cook spinach leaves over low heat 10 to 12 minutes or until spinach is reduced ⅔. Cool. In a blender, process spinach with ¼ cup Parmesan cheese., ⅓ cup Gruyère cheese, ⅓ cup yogurt and 2 eggs. Season with salt and pepper. In a blender, process apricots, remaining cheeses, yogurt and eggs.

Pour 1 inch (2.5 cm.) of spinach mixture in prepared pan. Spoon a layer of apricot mixture over spinach mixture. Alternate layers until pan is full. Place in a large baking pan. Pour boiling water in baking pan around mousse almost to top of loaf pan. Grease a sheet of waxed paper. Cover top of mousse with waxed paper. Bake in preheated oven 1 hour or until a knife inserted in center of mousse comes out clean. Cool completely. Unmold on a platter. Peel away waxed paper. Garnish with parsley. Makes 4 to 6 servings.

Per serving for 4: 320 kcal/26 g protein/16 g fat/17 g carbohydrate/18 g fiber

Tempura Vegetables

2 tablespoons whole-wheat flour
1 tablespoon all-purpose flour
½ teaspoon salt
2 egg whites
3 to 4 tablespoons water

Oil
2 lbs. fresh vegetables,
(mushrooms, cauliflower,
celery, fennel, onions, zucchini)
cut in serving pieces

To make batter, sift flours together. In a small bowl, mix flours and salt. Beat in egg whites. Gradually add water to mixture. In a medium saucepan, heat oil until smoking. Dip vegetables in batter. Deep fry 2 to 3 minutes. Drain on paper towels. Makes 4 servings.

Total recipe for batter: 350 kcal/8 g protein/30 g fat/13 g carbohydrate/ 2 g fiber

Tapénade

1 (8-oz.) jar black olives, pitted
⅓ cup capers
1 green chili, seeded, chopped
1 tablespoon soy sauce
2 tablespoons olive oil
Juice of 1 lemon
Freshly ground black pepper
Yolks of 2 hard-boiled eggs

To serve:
Whole-wheat bread, toasted, cut
  in serving pieces
Whole-wheat pita bread, cut in
  serving pieces

In a blender, process olives, capers, chili, soy sauce, oil, lemon juice and pepper to a thick purée. Spoon purée in center of a large platter. Crumble egg yolks over top.
  Serve surrounded with bread. Makes 4 servings.

Total recipe (excluding bread): 670 kcal/11 g protein/68 g fat/5 g carbohydrate/10 g fiber

Piperade

3 tablespoons olive oil
3 large green bell peppers, cored,
  seeded, coarsely chopped
2 large onions, chopped
2 large zucchini, chopped

1 lb. tomatoes, peeled
Salt
Pepper
4 eggs

In a medium skillet, heat oil. Add peppers, onions and zucchini. Sauté over low heat 20 minutes or until vegetables are soft. Add tomatoes. Cook 10 minutes or until vegetable mixture is a coarse purée. Season with salt and pepper. Stir and scramble eggs into mixture. Serve immediately. Makes 6 servings.

Per serving: 140 kcal/6 g protein/11 g fat/5 g carbohydrate/2 g fiber

Faiscedda

1 lb. fresh lima beans, shelled
1 tablespoon fresh summer
  savory, finely chopped
4 eggs, beaten
⅔ cup low-fat plain yogurt

Salt
Pepper

To serve:
Yogurt, if desired

Preheat oven to 400F (200C). Lightly grease 4 ramekins.

In a medium saucepan, boil beans in a small amount of water 10 minutes or until tender. If beans are old, remove outside skins after boiling. In a blender, process beans, summer savory, eggs and ⅔ cup yogurt. Season with salt and pepper.

Pour mixture into prepared ramekins. Bake in preheated oven 12 to 15 minutes or until all have risen. Serve with yogurt, if desired. Makes 4 servings.

Per serving: 150 kcal/12 g protein/7 g fat/10 g carbohydrate/5 g fiber

SOUPS

Good healthful soups are the easiest dishes to make in a cook's repertoire. However, there are a few important general rules to observe.

First, make sure that ingredients are in prime condition. Vegetables should be as fresh as possible for intensity of flavor and maximum mineral and vitamin content. Sauté prepared vegetables in a fine quality olive oil (buy extra virgin first pressing, if available).

Stock is the next important ingredient. Use vegetarian stock cubes or packaged soups. For stronger flavored soups made with legumes and winter vegetables, no stock is necessary. When needed, the best stock can be made from celery, onion and garlic. Chop one bunch of celery with two onions. Simmer celery and onions with various flavorings – bay leaves, parsley or garlic forty-five minutes. Crush vegetables with a potato masher. Cool; strain stock from vegetable debris. This liquid will keep, bottled in refrigerator, for a couple of weeks. Alternatively, make a good stock using outside leaves of any green vegetable on hand – cabbage, Brussels sprouts, cauliflower – chopped up with onions and carrots. Season and simmer in one cup (1.15 l.) water thirty minutes. Process in a blender, then sieve.

Soups can often be flavored at later stages of cooking with addition of one of the following: walnut or hazelnut oil, a good soy sauce like shoyu or tamari or flavored vinegars such as tarragon, basil or shallot. No recipe book can give a blueprint with precise amounts to insure the exact mixture of flavors. As with all cooking, tasting and checking flavors is the key to success.

Soups can be a delicious and satisfying meal in themselves when eaten with whole-wheat bread.

Tomato Soup $\boxed{\text{V}}$

3 lbs. tomatoes, pierced
⅔ cup dry sherry or vermouth
Salt
Pepper
1 tablespoon fresh basil, chopped, if desired

In a large saucepan, place tomatoes and sherry or vermouth. Season with salt and pepper. Cook, covered tightly, over very low heat 10 to 15 minutes or until tomatoes are reduced to a pulp. Cool. In a blender, process soup in batches until smooth. Strain through a sieve. Discard skin and pulp. Reheat soup. Sprinkle basil over top, if desired. Makes 6 servings.

Per serving: 60 kcal/2 g protein/negligible fat/7 g carbohydrate/ 3 g fiber

Garlic Soup

3 heads garlic
3 tablespoons extra virgin olive
   oil
7½ cups water
⅛ teaspoon saffron, if desired
Salt

Pepper
3 slices whole-wheat bread,
   cubed
Olive oil
2 tablespoons finely chopped fresh
   parsley

To make soup, break garlic cloves from heads. In a small bowl, cover garlic cloves with boiling water. Let stand 3 minutes. Peel. If cloves are big, cut in ½.

In a large saucepan, heat 3 tablespoons olive oil. Add garlic cloves. Cook 2 to 3 minutes. Add water and saffron, if desired. Season with salt and pepper. Simmer 1 hour. Cool. In a blender, process soup in batches until smooth.

In a medium skillet, fry bread in olive oil until crisp and brown. Reheat soup. Pour into warmed bowls. Top soup with croutons. Sprinkle parsley over top. Makes 6 servings.

Per serving: 225 kcal/3 g protein/19 g fat/12 g carbohydrate/3 g fiber

Chilled Avocado Soup

2 large ripe avocados, peeled,
   pitted, chopped
Grated peel and juice of 1 lemon
1 garlic clove, minced

Salt
Pepper
6¼ cups unsweetened soy milk

In a blender, process avocados, lemon peel and juice and garlic. Season with salt and pepper. Gradually add soy milk, processing to a thin purée. Refrigerate 1 hour. Makes 4 servings.

Per serving: 580 kcal/14 g protein/47 g fat/27 g carbohydrate/3 g fiber

Carrot Soup

2 tablespoons butter or
   margarine
1½ lbs. carrots, trimmed,
   chopped

7½ cups water
1 tablespoon raspberry vinegar
Salt
Pepper

In a large saucepan, melt butter or margarine. Add carrots. Cook 1 to 2 minutes. Add water. Simmer 30 minutes or until carrots are tender. Cool. In a blender, process soup to a purée. Blend in raspberry vinegar. Season with salt and pepper. Makes 6 servings.

Per serving: 60 kcal/1 g protein/4 g fat/6 g carbohydrate/4 g fiber

Chilled Sorrel Soup

½ lb. fresh sorrel leaves,
  trimmed
2 tablespoons butter or
  margarine
1 large onion, chopped

Salt
Pepper
7½ cups vegetable stock
  (page 43)
1 cup low-fat plain yogurt

In a large saucepan, melt butter or margarine. Add sorrel leaves and onion. Season with salt and pepper. Cook over low heat, covered, 5 minutes. Add celery or vegetable stock. Simmer 10 minutes. Cool. In a blender, process to a thin purée. Blend in yogurt. Refrigerate 1 hour. Makes 6 servings.

Per serving: 75 kcal/5 g protein/4 g fat/5 g carbohydrate/4 g fiber

Hot Avocado & Green Pepper Soup V

2 large ripe avocados, peeled,
  pitted, chopped
7½ cups vegetable stock
  (page 43)
2 large green bell peppers, cored,
  thinly sliced

2 tablespoons butter or
  margarine
Salt
Pepper

In a blender, process avocados and 3 cups vegetables stock to a purée. In a saucepan, cook peppers in butter or margarine, covered, 5 minutes. Add remaining vegetable stock. Simmer 10 minutes. Cool. In a blender, process mixture to a thin purée.

In a large saucepan, mix avocado and pepper purées. Season with salt and pepper. Reheat over low heat. Do not boil soup. Makes 4 servings.

Per serving: 395 kcal/7 g protein/39 g fat/4 g carbohydrate/4 g fiber

Beet & Ginger Soup I

⅓ cup peeled grated fresh
  gingerroot
2 tablespoons olive oil
1 lb. raw beets, peeled, chopped
1 onion, chopped

10 cups water
Salt
Pepper
⅔ cup low-fat plain yogurt

In a large saucepan, sauté ginger 1 to 2 minutes. Add beets, onion and water. Bring to a boil. Reduce heat. Simmer 2 hours. In a blender, process soup in batches until smooth. Return to pan. Season with salt and pepper. Reheat over low heat. Serve with yogurt. Makes 6 servings.

Per serving: 95 kcal/3 g protein/5 g fat/10 g carbohydrate/2 g fiber

Cream of Green Pea Soup

1 romaine lettuce heart, chopped
1 lb. fresh green peas, shelled
2 tablespoons butter or
   margarine
2½ cups water

5 cups skim milk or unsweetened
   soy milk
3 oz. tofu (bean curd)
Salt
Pepper

In a large saucepan, cook lettuce heart, peas and butter or margarine 1 to 2 minutes. Add water. Simmer 15 minutes; cool. Add milk and tofu. Season with salt and pepper. In a blender, process to a thin purée. Reheat over low heat to serve hot. Refrigerate to serve cold. Makes 6 servings.

Per serving: 160 kcal/12 g protein/5 g fat/18 g carbohydrate/4 g fiber

Thick Split Pea Soup

⅔ cup dried split green peas
2 tablespoons butter or
   margarine
1 tablespoon olive oil
2 onions, chopped

3 garlic cloves, minced
2 bay leaves
7½ cups celery stock (page 43)
Salt
Pepper

In a small bowl, cover peas with water. Soak 8 to 10 hours. Drain. Set aside. In a large saucepan, heat butter or margarine and oil. Add onions, garlic and bay leaves. Cook 1 to 2 minutes. Add peas and celery stock. Bring to a boil. Reduce heat.

Simmer 1 hour. Cool. Remove bay leaves. In a blender, process to a smooth thick purée. Season with salt and pepper. Reheat over low heat. Makes 6 servings.

Per serving: 135 kcal/6 g protein/6 g fat/15 g carbohydrate/3 g fiber

Navy Bean Soup

1½ cups dried navy beans
7½ cups water
2 tablespoons butter or
  margarine
2 tablespoons olive oil
2 medium onions, chopped

½ lb. fresh green beans, chopped
3 garlic cloves, minced
5 cups celery stock (page 43)
Salt
Pepper

In a large bowl, cover navy beans with water. Soak 8 to 10 hours. In a large saucepan, cook navy beans and liquid 2 hours or until tender. Add water as needed. Set aside. In a large saucepan, heat butter or margarine and oil. Add onions, green beans and garlic. Cook 1 to 2 minutes. Add celery stock. Simmer 20 minutes.

In a blender, process ½ of navy beans and liquid to a smooth purée. Mix purée with remaining navy beans and liquid. Add vegetables and stock. Reheat, stirring carefully. Season with salt and pepper. Makes 6 servings.

Per serving: 200 kcal/13 g protein/4 g fat/29 g carbohydrate/16 g fiber

Green Winter Soup

1 cup dried navy beans
2 tablespoons butter or
  margarine
1 small green cabbage, chopped
4 garlic cloves, minced
7½ cups vegetable stock (page
  43)

Salt
Pepper
1 large bunch fresh parsley, stems
  removed

In a medium bowl, cover beans with water. Soak 2 to 3 hours. In a medium saucepan, simmer beans and liquid 1 hour or until tender. Drain. Set aside. In a large saucepan, melt butter or margarine. Add cabbage and garlic. Cook over low heat 5 minutes. Add 5 cups vegetable stock. Simmer 20 minutes. Add beans to vegetable mixture. Season with salt and pepper.

In a blender, process remaining vegetable stock and parsley to a purée. Add to soup. Reheat, stirring carefully. Makes 6 servings.

Per serving: 150 kcal/10 g protein/4 g fat/20 g carbohydrate/12 g fiber

Beet & Ginger Soup II

1 lb. raw beets, peeled, chopped	Salt
1 small white cabbage, chopped	Pepper
5 garlic cloves, minced	Boiling water
⅓ cup peeled grated fresh gingerroot	⅔ cup low-fat plain yogurt

Preheat oven to 350F (175C).

In a 9-inch-square baking dish, mix beets, cabbage, garlic and ginger. Season with salt and pepper. Cover vegetables with 1½ inches boiling water. Bake in preheated oven 2½ to 3 hours.

Remove dish from oven. Pour off liquid. Discard vegetables. Serve with yogurt. Makes 6 servings.

Per serving: 65 kcal/4 g protein/negligible fat/12 g carbohydrate/6 g fiber

Fennel & Orange Soup

2 fennel roots	3 tablespoons ouzo or anise liqueur
Boiling water	
6 oranges	Salt
2 garlic cloves, minced	Pepper

Cut feathery leaves from fennel roots and chop; reserve. In a medium bowl, grate roots. Cover roots with boiling water. Cool. Reserve 1 orange. Squeeze juice from remaining oranges. Add orange juice and garlic to fennel. Grate peel from remaining orange. Add to fennel. Peel orange, removing all pith. Slice orange crosswise thinly; float in soup. Add ouzo or anise liqueur to soup. Season with salt and pepper. Stir well. Refrigerate 1 hour. Pour into a soup tureen. To decorate, top with reserved fennel leaves. Makes 4 servings.

Per serving: 125 kcal/4 g protein/negligible fat/23 g carbohydrate/8 g fiber

---

Beet & Ginger Soup II (*above*), Fennel & Orange Soup

Spinach Soup

1 lb. fresh leaf spinach, trimmed
2 tablespoons butter or
    margarine
¾ cup shredded Cheddar cheese
⅛ teaspoon sage

5 cups vegetable stock (page 43)
2½ cups unsweetened soy milk
Salt
Pepper

In a large saucepan, cook spinach leaves in butter or margarine over low heat, covered, 5 minutes. Add cheese, sage and vegetable stock. Simmer 5 minutes. Cool. In a blender, process mixture to a thin purée. Blend in soy milk. Season with salt and pepper. Reheat over low heat. Makes 4 servings.

Per serving: 330 kcal/15 g protein/25 g fat/11 g carbohydrate/7 g fiber

Macaroni & Bean Soup   V

1 cup dried navy beans
Water
3 tablespoons olive oil
1 onion, finely chopped
2 garlic cloves, minced
1 bunch celery, finely chopped
1 teaspoon rosemary

1 teaspoon oregano
1 tablespoon tomato purée
1½ cups whole-wheat macaroni
Salt
Pepper
Vegetable stock (page 43), if
    desired

In a large bowl, cover beans with water. Soak 8 to 10 hours. In a large saucepan, cook beans and liquid 2 hours or until tender. Add water, if needed. In a blender, process ½ of beans and enough cooking liquid to obtain a purée. Set aside.

In a large saucepan, heat oil. Add onion, garlic, celery, rosemary and oregano. Cook over low heat 5 minutes. Add remaining beans and cooking liquid, tomato purée and macaroni. Simmer 10 minutes. Season with salt and pepper. Add bean purée. Reheat over low heat, stirring well. Add vegetable stock, if desired, to make a thinner soup. Makes 6 servings.

Per serving: 310 kcal/15 g protein/9 g fat/45 g carbohydrate/16 g fiber

---

Stuffed Artichoke (*above*, page 36), Spinach & Apricot Mousse (*center*, page 40), Cheese Bites (*below*, page 32)

SALADS

Almost any vegetable can be eaten raw: chopped, diced, grated and occasionally blanched, then tossed in dressing. Not only are vegetables delicious raw, they also retain all the essential nutrients which are so often lost in cooking. Salads are made from a large range of vegetables in season, combining with fresh and dried fruits, nuts, grains and legumes.

To achieve successful salads, the first essential is to buy the very freshest ingredients. If you have a garden, there is no problem. Leaves picked in a vegetable garden, then immediately dressed and tossed in a salad, have a density of flavor never apparent in leaves bought in a market.

For salad enthusiasts there is now a greater range of salad vegetables on the market. Butter lettuce, Italian chicory and Belgian endive can all be found in markets. These, as well as many more delicious and unusual vegetables, can be grown in our gardens.

Even if these more obscure vegetables are beyond reach, you can still make exciting salads from the vegetables which are in season. A salad of raw vegetables eaten once a day is good for health. Many salads can be entire summer meals and many of the winter salads would also make a tempting light lunch.

Green Salad

1 head romaine lettuce
½ cup fresh dandelion greens
1 bunch fresh watercress
1 bunch fresh parsley, trimmed
2 to 3 fresh sorrel leaves, trimmed

1 tablespoon lemon juice
2 tablespoons walnut oil
1 tablespoon low-fat plain yogurt
Salt
Pepper

In a large bowl, arrange lettuce leaves around sides. Place dandelion greens, watercress and parsley in center of bowl. Sprinkle with sorrel leaves. To make dressing, in a small bowl mix lemon juice, oil and yogurt. Season with salt and pepper. Pour over center of salad just before serving. Makes 4 servings.

Per serving: 80 kcal/2 g protein/8 g fat/1 g carbohydrate/2 g fiber

Stuffed Artichoke (*top*, page 36), Spinach & Apricot Mousse (*center*, page 40), Cheese Bites (*bottom*, page 32)

Spinach, Sorrel & Avocado Salad   ⟦V⟧

½ lb. fresh young spinach leaves,
    trimmed
4 oz. fresh young sorrel leaves,
    trimmed
2 ripe avocados, peeled, pitted,
    sliced

2 garlic cloves, minced
Grated peel and juice of 1 lemon
2 tablespoons walnut oil
Salt
Pepper
½ cup pistachio nuts

In a large bowl, arrange spinach and sorrel leaves around sides and bottom. In a medium bowl, toss avocado, garlic, lemon peel and juice and oil. Season with salt and pepper. Just before serving, mound avocado mixture in bottom of large bowl. Sprinkle pistachio nuts over top. Makes 4 servings.

Per serving: 355 kcal/10 g protein/32 g fat/8 g carbohydrate/9 g fiber

Pepper Salad   ⟦V⟧

1 tablespoon fresh parsley,
    chopped
½ cup nasturtium leaves,
    chopped
2 green bell peppers, cored, seeded,
    finely sliced
2 red bell peppers, cored, seeded,
    finely sliced
2 yellow bell peppers, cored,
    seeded, finely sliced

1 tablespoon green peppercorns
Grated peel and juice of 1 lemon
2 tablespoons olive oil
Salt
Pepper

To decorate:
6 nasturtium flowers

On a large platter, sprinkle ½ of parsley and nasturtium leaves. Arrange green, red and yellow peppers in strips across platter. To make dressing, in a small bowl, mix green peppercorns and lemon peel and juice. Add oil. Season with salt and pepper. Stir well. Pour dressing over sliced peppers. Sprinkle remaining parsley and nasturtium leaves over peppers. Decorate with nasturtium flowers. Makes 4 servings.

Per serving: 95 kcal/2 g protein/8 g fat/4 g carbohydrate/2 g fiber

Tomato & Basil Salad

2 lbs. tomatoes, thinly sliced
1 large bunch fresh basil leaves,
  coarsely chopped
1 tablespoon red wine vinegar

2 tablespoons olive oil
Salt
Pepper

In a large dish, layer tomatoes. Cover tomatoes with basil. To make dressing, in a small bowl, mix vinegar and oil. Season with salt and pepper. Pour over tomatoes just before serving. Makes 4 servings.

Per serving: 105 kcal/2 g protein/8 g fat/7 g carbohydrate/4 g fiber

Zucchini Salad

2 lbs. young zucchini, trimmed,
  grated
1 bunch fresh mint, chopped
1 teaspoon lemon juice

2 tablespoons olive oil
Salt
Pepper

In a large bowl, combine zucchini, mint, lemon juice and oil. Season with salt and pepper. Makes 4 servings.

Per serving: 115 kcal/2 g protein/8 g fat/9 g carbohydrate/4 g fiber

Snow Pea Salad

1 lb. fresh snow peas, trimmed,
  halved
1⅓ cups buckwheat groats,
  toasted
1 bunch green onions, coarsely
  chopped

Grated peel and juice of 1 lemon
2 tablespoons olive oil
Salt
Pepper

In a large saucepan, blanch snow peas in boiling water 1 minute. In a large bowl, combine snow peas, buckwheat groats, onions, lemon peel and juice and oil. Season with salt and pepper. Makes 4 servings.

Per serving: 280 kcal/9 g protein/9 g fat/44 g carbohydrate/8 g fiber

Mushroom, Onion & Walnut Salad

1 lb. fresh mushrooms, wiped
  clean
2 large onions, thinly sliced
½ cup walnuts, crushed

1 tablespoon red wine vinegar
2 tablespoons walnut oil
Salt
Pepper

Discard tough mushrooms stalks. Slice mushrooms crosswise. In a large bowl, combine mushrooms, onions and walnuts. Toss well. To make dressing, in a small bowl, mix vinegar and oil. Season with salt and pepper. Pour over salad. Marinate 1 hour. Makes 4 servings.

Per serving; 162 kcal/4 g protein/15 g fat/3 g carbohydrate/4 g fiber

Beet Salad

2 lbs. raw beets, peeled, grated
2 large onions, grated
2 garlic cloves, minced
Grated peel and juice of 1 lemon
2 tablespoons olive oil

1 teaspoon umbushi or tarragon
  vinegar
Salt
Pepper

In a large bowl, combine beets, onions, garlic and lemon juice and peel. To make dressing, in a small bowl, mix oil and umbushi or tarragon vinegar. Season with salt and pepper. Pour over salad. Mix well. Makes 6 servings.

Per serving: 130 kcal/4 g protein/5 g fat/19 g carbohydrate/5 g fiber

Celery & Artichoke Salad   [V]

12 artichoke hearts
1 lb. new potatoes
2 celery hearts, finely chopped
2 garlic cloves, minced

Grated peel and juice of 1 lemon
2 tablespoons olive oil
Salt
Pepper

Remove outer leaves from artichokes; discard. In a large saucepan, cover artichokes with water. Boil 15 minutes or until tender. Using a slotted spoon, remove artichokes. Drain well. Remove artichoke hearts. Discard leaves. Boil potatoes in artichoke water 20 minutes or until tender. Drain well. Quarter artichokes and potatoes. In a large bowl, combine artichokes and potatoes. Add celery hearts.

    To make dressing, in a small bowl, mix garlic, lemon peel and juice and oil. Season with salt and pepper. Pour over salad. Makes 6 servings.

Per serving: 125 kcal/3 g protein/5 g fat/18 g carbohydrate/4 g fiber

Celeriac Salad

1 large celeriac root, peeled,
  grated
2 large onions, grated
2 garlic cloves, minced
2 tablespoons olive oil

1 tablespoon white wine vinegar
Salt
Pepper
3 tablespoons fresh parsley,
  chopped

In a large bowl, pour boiling water over celeriac root. Let stand 1 minute.
Drain carefully. Add onions, garlic, oil and vinegar. Season with salt and
pepper. Toss well. Sprinkle parsley over top. Makes 4 servings.

Per serving: 105 kcal/3 g protein/7 g fat/8 g carbohydrate/4 g fiber

Potato & Celeriac

2 lbs. new potatoes
1 large celeriac root, peeled, diced
  in 1-inch (2.5 cm.) cubes
1 bunch green onions, coarsely
  chopped
2 tablespoons capers

2 tablespoons olive oil
Grated peel and juice of 1 lemon
⅔ cup low-fat plain yogurt
Salt
Pepper

In a large saucepan, cover potatoes with water. Boil until tender. Drain
well; cool. Cut in quarters. In a large saucepan, steam celeriac cubes 10
to 15 minutes or until tender. Cool. In a large bowl, combine potatoes and
celeriac cubes. Add onions and capers. In a small bowl, mix oil, lemon peel
and juice and yogurt. Season with salt and pepper. Pour over vegetables.
Toss thoroughly. Makes 4 servings.

Per serving: 280 kcal/8 g protein/8 g fat/47 g carbohydrate/11 g fiber

Green Bean Salad

1 cup dried navy beans
Salt
Pepper
2 tablespoons olive oil
2 garlic cloves, minced
Grated peel and juice of 1 lemon

1 lb. fresh green beans, cut in ½-
  inch (1.5 cm.) pieces
1 lb. fresh lima beans, shelled
¼ cup fresh mint, finely
  chopped

In a large bowl, cover beans with water. Soak 2 hours. In a large saucepan,
boil beans and liquid 45 minutes or until tender. Drain well. In a large
bowl, season navy beans with salt and pepper. Add oil, garlic and lemon
peel and juice. In a large saucepan, cover green beans and lima beans with
water. Boil 5 minutes. Drain. Add to navy beans. Mix thoroughly. Makes
6 servings.

Per serving: 190 kcal/10 g protein/12 g fat/12 g carbohydrate/6 g fiber

Tuscan Bean Salad   V

½ cup dried navy beans
½ cup dried red kidney beans
½ cup dried black beans
1 tablespoon dried oregano
1 lb. fresh green beans, trimmed,
   chopped
1 lb. fresh lima beans, shelled
1 bunch fresh mint, finely
   chopped
1 bunch fresh chives, finely
   chopped
1 bunch fresh fennel leaves, finely
   chopped
1 tablespoon red wine vinegar
2 tablespoons olive oil
3 garlic cloves, minced
Salt
Pepper

In a medium bowl, cover navy beans, red kidney beans and black beans with water. Soak 8 to 10 hours. Drain. In a medium saucepan, cover soaked beans with water. Add oregano. Boil 10 minutes. Reduce heat. Simmer 1½ hours or until tender. Cool. Drain well.

In a large saucepan, boil or steam green beans and lima beans until just tender. Drain well. In a large bowl, combine all cooked beans. Add mint, chives, fennel leaves, vinegar, oil and garlic. Season with salt and pepper. Stir well. Marinate 1 hour. Makes 6 servings.

Per serving: 260 kcal/17 g protein/7 g fat/34 g carbohydrate/21 g fiber

✳ Rice & Vegetable Salad   V

1 small cauliflower, thinly sliced
1 bunch green onions, coarsely
   chopped
2 green bell peppers, cored, seeded,
   thinly sliced
2 small turnips, grated
2 small carrots, grated
1⅓ cups cooked brown or white
   long-grain rice
2 garlic cloves, minced
Grated peel and juice of 1 lemon
2 tablespoons olive oil
1 tablespoon red wine vinegar
Salt
Pepper

Crumble cauliflower florets. In a large bowl, mix cauliflower, onions, peppers, turnips, carrots and rice thoroughly. Add garlic and lemon peel and juice, then oil and vinegar. Season with salt and pepper. Mix well. Let stand 15 minutes. Makes 6 servings.

Per serving: 120 kcal/3 g protein/5 g fat/16 g carbohydrate/4 g fiber

Winter Salad

$\boxed{V}$

1 white cabbage, trimmed,
    grated
4 large carrots, grated
2 large cooking apples, cored,
    grated
1 large onion, grated
1 fennel root, grated
2 green bell peppers, cored, seeded,
    thinly sliced

Grated peel of 1 lemon
Juice of 1 lemon
2 garlic cloves, minced
1 teaspoon prepared mustard
2 tablespoons olive oil
Salt
Pepper

In a large bowl, combine cabbage, carrots, apples, onions, fennel root, peppers and lemon peel. To make dressing, in a small bowl, mix lemon juice, garlic, mustard and oil. Season with salt and pepper. Pour over salad. Toss well. Let stand 10 minutes. Makes 6 servings.

Per serving: 135 kcal/5 g protein/5 g fat/18 g carbohydrate/9 g fiber

PIES, TARTS, QUICHES & BREADS

This chapter offers recipes for various types of savory pastries, as well as different breads. There are recipes for tarts, pies and quiches. These names have been blurred by misuse and today, especially in vegetarian cooking, can mean anything. Even traditionally pie doesn't necessarily imply pastry – neither cottage pie nor shepherds' pie contains pastry. Here pie is defined in the old English sense of food cooked in a sauce and encased completely by pastry which both keeps in and soaks up flavor. Vegetarian Lenten pies of Mediterranean countries are famous. A tart can be defined as not containing eggs but using cream or cheese to thicken, as in the French classic dish, *Tarte à l'oignon*. A quiche uses cream, eggs and cheese. However, these definitions are no longer used precisely. To avoid overusing saturated fats, these ingredients are kept to a minimum while retaining the true character of the recipes.

For pastry, whole-wheat flour is used. If fats are not mixed well into whole-wheat flour, it can be heavy. Perhaps a mixture of half all-purpose flour and half whole-wheat flour would suit some palates better. This is very much a personal choice. In a vegetarian diet you get enough dietary fiber to not need whole-wheat flour in every dish, though for flavor it is always best. A recipe is given for a high protein loaf, which is packed with goodness, and two recipes for more unusual breads, one of which uses all-purpose flour.

Cauliflower & Fennel Pie $\boxed{V}$

2 recipes Whole-Wheat Pastry,
   Zucchini Tart (page 65)
1 small cauliflower, broken in
   florets
2 heads fresh fennel, trimmed,
   quartered
1 large onion, cut in chunks
2 tablespoons butter or
   margarine

4 tablespoons all-purpose flour
1¾ cups vegetable stock (page
   43)
2 tablespoons soy sauce
1 tablespoon Dijon-style
   mustard
Freshly ground black pepper

Preheat oven to 400F (200C). Grease a 3-inch deep pie dish.

Make pastry as directed, page 65. Line prepared pie dish with ⅔ of pastry. In a large saucepan, boil cauliflowerets, fennel and onion in a small amount of water 5 minutes or until tender. Drain. Arrange vegetables in pastry shell, packing tightly. In a medium saucepan, melt butter or margarine. Stir in flour to make a roux. In a small bowl, mix vegetable stock, soy sauce and mustard. Add mixture slowly to roux. Season with pepper. Pour sauce over vegetables in pastry shell.

On a lightly floured surface, roll out remaining pastry. Cover pie with pastry, pressing edges together firmly. Grease a piece of waxed paper. Cover top of pie with waxed paper. Bake in preheated oven 40 minutes. Remove waxed paper after 30 minutes. Makes 6 servings.

Per serving: 365 kcal/9 g protein/23 g fat/33 g carbohydrate/8 g fiber

Swiss Chard Pie

Photograph, page 67

2 recipes Whole-Wheat Pastry,
  Zucchini Tart (page 65)
1 lb. fresh Swiss chard, coarsely
  chopped
⅛ teaspoon grated nutmeg
2 tablespoons butter or
  margarine

¼ cup all-purpose flour
1¼ cups low-fat milk
¼ cup shredded Gruyère cheese
⅔ cup grated Parmesan cheese
Salt
Pepper
4 eggs, hard-boiled, halved

Preheat oven to 350F (175C). Grease a 3-inch deep pie dish.

Make pastry as directed, page 65. Line prepared pie dish with ⅔ of pastry. In a large saucepan, cook Swiss chard, covered, 12 minutes. Cool. In a blender, process Swiss chard and nutmeg to a coarse purée.

In a medium saucepan, melt butter or margarine. Stir in flour to make a roux. Add milk, Gruyère cheese and Parmesan cheese. Season with salt and pepper. Combine sauce and Swiss chard. Mix thoroughly. Pour mixture into pastry shell. Push eggs into filling at intervals.

On a lightly floured surface, roll out remaining pastry. Cover pie with pastry, pressing edges together firmly. Grease a piece of waxed paper. Cover top of pie with waxed paper. Bake in preheated oven 50 minutes. Remove waxed paper after 38 minutes. Makes 6 servings.

Per serving: 500 kcal/21 g protein/33 g fat/32 g carbohydrate/9 g fiber

Eggplant & Bean Pie   V

⅓ cup dried red kidney beans
1 large eggplant, thinly sliced
2 tablespoons olive oil
1½ lbs. tomatoes, peeled
3 tablespoons tomato purée
2 tablespoons soy sauce

3 tablespoons fresh basil, finely
   chopped
Salt
Pepper
2 recipes Whole-Wheat Pastry,
   Zucchini Tart (page 65)

In a small bowl, cover beans with water. Soak 8 to 10 hours. In a small saucepan, boil beans and water 10 minutes. Drain. Cover beans with clean water. Simmer beans 1½ hours or until tender. Drain. Set aside. In a large bowl, sprinkle salt on egg plant. Let stand 1 hour.

Preheat oven to 350F (175C). Grease a 3-inch deep pie dish.

Rinse eggplant thoroughly under cold running water. Pat dry. In a large skillet, heat oil. Add eggplant. Fry briefly on both sides. In a large saucepan, cook tomatoes over low heat, covered, 5 minutes. Add tomato purée, soy sauce and basil. Season with salt and pepper. In a large bowl, mix beans, eggplant and tomato sauce.

Make pastry as directed. Line prepared pie dish with ⅔ of pastry. Fill pastry shell with vegetable mixture. On a lightly floured surface, roll out remaining pastry. Cover pie with pastry, pressing edges together firmly. Grease a piece of waxed paper. Cover top of pie with waxed paper. Bake in preheated oven 50 minutes. Removed waxed paper after 38 minutes. Makes 6 servings.

Per serving: 415 kcal/11 g protein/25 g fat/39g carbohydrate/11 g fiber

Zucchini Tart

Whole-Wheat Pastry:
⅞ cup whole-wheat flour
½ teaspoon baking powder
½ teaspoon salt
¼ cup butter or margarine
2 tablespoons corn oil
2 to 3 tablespoons water

Filling:
2 tablespoons butter or
    margarine
1 lb. zucchini, diced

1 small onion, chopped
1 tablespoon chopped fresh
    tarragon
1 tablespoon chopped fresh
    parsley
2 eggs
⅔ cup low-fat plain yogurt
⅓ cup grated Parmesan cheese
Salt
Pepper

Whole-Wheat Pastry
In a medium bowl, mix flour, baking powder and salt. With a pastry blender or 2 knives, cut in butter or margarine until mixture resembles coarse crumbs. Add oil and water slowly, making a stiff paste. Wrap in plastic wrap or waxed paper. Refrigerate 1 hour. Remove pastry from refrigerator. Let stand until pastry is room temperature.

Preheat oven to 400F (200C).

On a lightly floured surface, roll out dough to an 11-inch circle. Line a 9-inch pie dish with pastry. Line pastry with foil. Fill with pie weights or dried beans. Bake in preheated oven 5 to 8 minutes, or until pastry is golden. Remove foil and beans.

Adjust oven to 350F (180C). To make filling, in a large skillet, melt butter or margarine. Add zucchini, onion, tarragon and parsley. Cook over medium heat 5 minutes. Cool. Beat in eggs, yogurt and Parmesan cheese. Season with salt and pepper. Pour mixture into prepared pastry shell. Bake in preheated oven 40 minutes. Serve hot or cold. Makes 6 servings.

Per serving: 245 kcal/8 g protein/16 g fat/18g carbohydrate/4 g fiber

Mushroom Tart

1 (9-inch) Whole-Wheat Pastry
   shell, Zucchini Tart (page 65)
2 tablespoons butter or
   margarine
1 lb. fresh mushrooms, sliced
2 medium onions, sliced

⅓ cup grated Parmesan cheese
¼ cup shredded Gruyère cheese
1 bunch green onions, chopped
1 cup low-fat plain yogurt
Salt
Pepper

Preheat oven to 425F (218C). Make pastry as directed. Set aside.

In a large saucepan, melt butter or margarine. Add mushrooms and onions. Cook over low heat 5 minutes. Cool. Add Parmesan cheese, Gruyère cheese, green onions and yogurt. Season with salt and pepper. Stir thoroughly. Spoon mixture into prepared pastry shell. Bake in preheated oven 30 minutes. Makes 6 servings.

Per serving: 245 kcal/8 g protein/16 g fat/18 g carbohydrate/4 g fiber

Onion Tart

1 (9-inch) Whole-Wheat Pastry
   shell, Zucchini Tart (page 65)
1 tablespoon butter or
   margarine
4 medium onions, chopped
1 egg

⅔ cup skim milk
2 tablespoons green peppercorns
⅛ teaspoon grated nutmeg
Salt
Pepper
12 black olives, pitted, sliced

Preheat oven to 350F (175C). Make pastry as directed. Set aside.

In a medium saucepan, melt butter or margarine. Add onions. Cook 10 minutes or until soft. In a small bowl, beat egg and milk. Mix with onions. Add peppercorns and nutmeg. Season with salt and pepper. Mix thoroughly. Pour into prepared pastry shell. Arrange olives on tart. Bake in preheated oven 40 minutes. Makes 6 servings.

Per serving: 200 kcal/6 g protein/12 g fat/18 g carbohydrate/3 g fiber

Swiss Chard Pie (*above*, page 63), Onion Tart

Pepper & Leek Tart

1 (9-inch) Whole-Wheat Pastry
  shell, Zucchini Tart (page 65)
4 tablespoons butter or
  margarine
3 green bell peppers, cored, seeded,
  coarsely chopped
1 lb. leeks, chopped

1 egg
1¼ cups skim milk
3 tablespoons fresh parsley,
  chopped
Salt
Pepper

Preheat oven to 350F (175C). Make pastry as directed. Set aside.

In a medium saucepan, melt butter or margarine. Add peppers and leeks. Cook, covered, 15 minutes. In a small bowl, beat egg and milk. Add to peppers and leeks. Mix thoroughly. Add parsley. Season with salt and pepper. Pour into prepared pastry shell. Bake in preheated oven 40 minutes. Makes 6 servings.

Per serving: 270 kcal/7 g protein/18g fat/21 g carbohydrate/5 g fiber

Roquefort Quiche

1 (9-inch) Whole-Wheat Pastry
  shell, Zucchini Tart (page 65)
1½ cups crumbled Roquefort
  cheese
1 (3-oz.) pkg. Neufchâtel cheese
⅓ cup cottage cheese
3 tablespoons low-fat plain
  yogurt

1 bunch fresh parsley, chopped
1 bunch green onions, chopped
2 egg whites
1 egg
Salt
Pepper

Preheat oven to 375F (190C). Make pastry as directed. Set aside.

In a medium bowl, mix Roquefort cheese, Neufchâtel cheese, cottage cheese and yogurt. Add parsley and onions. Beat egg whites and 1 egg into mixture. Season with salt and pepper. Pour mixture into prepared pastry shell. Bake 30 to 40 minutes. Makes 6 servings.

Per serving: 315 kcal/14 g protein/23 g fat/14 g carbohydrate/2 g fiber

Corn Bread (*above*, page 72), Roquefort Quiche

Tomato & Oatmeal Tart

1 cup regular rolled oats
⅞ cup whole-wheat flour
½ teaspoon salt
⅓ cup butter or margarine
1 egg, beaten
1½ lbs. tomatoes
4 garlic cloves, minced

1 small chili, seeded, chopped
⅓ cup grated Parmesan cheese
¼ cup shredded Gruyère cheese
1 egg
Salt
Pepper

To make crust, in a medium bowl, mix oats, flour and salt. With a pastry blender or 2 knives, cut in butter or margarine. Add egg. Refrigerate 1 hour. Remove pastry from refrigerator. Let stand until pastry is room temperature. Preheat oven to 350F (175C). On a lightly floured surface, roll out pastry to an 11-inch circle. Line a 9-inch pie dish with pastry. Line pastry with foil. Fill with pie weights or dried beans. Bake in preheated oven 5 to 8 minutes or until pastry is golden. Remove foil and beans.

To make filling, in a large saucepan, cook tomatoes, garlic and chili over low heat 10 to 15 minutes. Strain through a sieve; discard skins. Add Parmesan cheese and Gruyère cheese to tomato purée. Beat in egg. Season with salt and pepper. Pour into prepared pastry shell. Place tart on a baking sheet. Bake 30 to 35 minutes. Makes 6 servings.

Per serving: 320 kcal/11 g protein/18 g fat/30 g carbohydrate/5 g fiber

Spinach Quiche

1 (9-inch) Whole-Wheat Pastry
   shell, Zucchini Tart (page 65)
1 lb. fresh leaf spinach, trimmed
½ (8-oz.) pkg. Neufchâtel cheese
1 cup shredded Cheddar cheese

⅔ cup grated Parmesan cheese
⅛ teaspoon nutmeg
Salt
4 eggs

Preheat oven to 400F (200C). Make pastry as directed. Set aside.

In a medium saucepan, cook spinach until bulk is reduced ⅔. Remove from heat. Cool. Add Neufchâtel cheese, Cheddar cheese, Parmesan cheese and nutmeg. Season with salt. Beat eggs into mixture. Gently pour into prepared pastry shell. Bake in preheated oven 30 minutes. Makes 6 servings.

Per serving: 350 kcal/21 g protein/24 g fat/14 g carbohydrate/8 g fiber

Quiche au Ratatouille

1 (9-inch) Whole-Wheat Pastry
   shell, Zucchini Tart (page 65)
1 eggplant, sliced in ¼-inch
   pieces
4 tablespoons olive oil
2 green bell peppers, cored,
   seeded
2 zucchini, chopped
2 onions, chopped
5 garlic cloves, minced
1 lb. tomatoes, peeled
Salt
Pepper
3 tablespoons fresh parsley,
   chopped
3 eggs
½ cup shredded Cheddar cheese

Make pastry as directed. Set aside.

In a large bowl, sprinkle eggplant with salt. Let stand 1 hour. Rinse well under cold running water. Pat dry. Preheat oven to 425F (218C).

In a large skillet, heat oil. Add eggplant, peppers, zucchini, onions and garlic. Cook over low heat 15 minutes. Add tomatoes. Cook 10 minutes. Season with salt and pepper. Stir in parsley. Remove from heat. When cool, beat in eggs and cheese. Pour mixture into prepared pastry shell. Bake 30 minutes. Makes 6 servings.

Per serving: 350 kcal/10 g protein/26 g fat/21 g carbohydrate/6 g fiber

High Protein Loaf

2 (¼-oz.) pkgs. active dry yeast
3 to 4 cups warm water
8 cups whole-wheat flour
1 teaspoon sea salt
3 tablespoons cracked wheat
3 tablespoons soy flour
3 tablespoons bran
¼ cup wheat germ
3 tablespoons sesame seeds
1 tablespoon dried brewers' yeast
½ cup non-fat dry milk powder
3 tablespoons olive oil
2 tablespoons molasses
1 tablespoon dried malt extract

Grease 3 (9" × 5") loaf pans. In a large bowl, dissolve yeast in 2 to 3 tablespoons of warm water. Let stand 5 to 10 minutes or until foamy. Add whole-wheat flour, sea salt, cracked wheat, soy flour, bran, wheat germ, sesame seeds, brewers' yeast and milk powder. Mix thoroughly. Add olive oil, molasses and malt extract. Mix thoroughly. Gradually add enough warm water to make dough elastic throughout. Dough should be tacky. Do not knead. Divide dough evenly among prepared loaf pans. Slip pans in plastic bags. Let stand in a warm place 1 hour or until dough doubles in bulk.

Preheat oven to 450F (275C). Bake in preheated oven 15 minutes. Adjust oven to 350F (175C). Bake 20 minutes. Remove from pans. Cool on wire racks. Makes 3 loaves.

Total recipe: 4890 kcal/204 g protein/120 g fat/803 g carbohydrate/116 g fiber
Per slice (12 slices per loaf): 135 kcal/6 g protein/3 g fat/22 g carbohydrate/ 3 g fiber

Corn Bread

Photograph, page 68

2 tablespoons butter or
   margarine
2 onions, chopped
1 (12-oz.) can whole kernel corn
1⅓ cups cornmeal
1 teaspoon sea salt

1¼ cups low-fat milk
1 cup shredded Gruyère cheese
1 cup cottage cheese
6 eggs, separated
1 teaspoon dried anise seed

Preheat oven to 400F (200C). Grease 3 (9" × 5") loaf pans.
   In a small saucepan, melt butter or margarine. Add onions. Cook until
soft. Set aside. In a large bowl, mix corn, cornmeal, salt and milk. Add
onions, Gruyère cheese and cottage cheese. Blend well. Add egg yolks and
anise seed. Beat well. In a medium bowl, beat egg whites until stiff. Fold
into mixture. Pour mixture in prepared loaf pans. Bake 45 minutes. Cool
on wire racks. Makes 3 loaves.

*Total recipe: 2330 kcal/115 g protein/111 g fat/233 g carbohydrate/17 g
fiber*
*Per slice (12 slices per loaf): 65 kcal/3 g protein/3 g fat/6 g carbohydrate/
1 g fiber*

Fruit Loaf

$\boxed{\text{V}}$

1¾ cups all-purpose flour
1½ teaspoons baking powder
1 teaspoon salt
¾ cup golden raisins
⅓ cup chopped dates
⅓ cup currants
1 teaspoon grated nutmeg

1 teaspoon pumpkin pie spice
1¼ cups low-fat milk or
   unsweetened soy milk
2 tablespoons dried malt extract
1 tablespoon molasses
1 tablespoon honey

Preheat oven to 325F (150C). Grease a 9" × 5" loaf pan.
   In a large bowl, sift flour, baking powder and salt together. Add raisins,
dates, currants, nutmeg and pumpkin pie spice. In a small saucepan, heat
milk, malt extract, molasses and honey over low heat until lukewarm and
well mixed. Pour into flour and dried fruit mixture. Using a wooden
spoon, beat mixture to a soft dough. Press dough into prepared loaf pan.
Bake 1 hour. Cool on a wire rack.

Total recipe: 1570 kcal/44 g protein/10 g fat/347 g carbohydrate/38 g fiber
*Per slice (12 slices per loaf): 130 kcal/4g protein/1 g fat/29 g carbohydrate/
3 g fiber*

BEAN DISHES

These dishes are considered to be staple vegetarian food. To some degree they have done harm to the idea of vegetarian cuisine being considered gourmet because they have bequeathed the stigma of being stodgy and bland. In fact there is a lot of truth to the idea. Light, airy meals cannot be prepared with a lot of beans and grains. However, a little of each complement other dishes. It is a matter of balance and harmony – which is what the art of cooking is about as much as any other art.

The legume family needs flavoring to lift their earthiness. Use plenty of fresh herbs. If not available, use dried herbs and spices. Use flavored oils like walnut and sesame oils to start the cooking, or add a tablespoon at the end. Even flavored vinegars can help. One of the best additions in cooking legumes is the peel of lemon, orange or tamarind. One of these with bay leaves or a sprig of rosemary adds flavor.

Baked Beans

¾ cup dried navy beans
1 (14-oz.) can tomatoes
3 tablespoons tomato purée
1 tablespoon brown sugar

¼ cup kosher margarine
Water
Salt
Pepper

In a small bowl, cover beans with water. Soak 8 to 10 hours. Preheat oven to 325F (150C). In a medium saucepan, boil beans and water 10 minutes. Drain well. In a 1-quart baking dish, combine beans, tomatoes, tomato purée, brown sugar and margarine. Add enough water to cover beans 1½ inches. Bake, tightly covered, 3½ hours or until beans are tender. Season with salt and pepper. Makes 4 servings.

Per serving: 180 kcal/10 g protein/5 g fat/25 g carbohydrate/5 g fiber

Caribbean Black Beans [V]

1 cup dried black beans
2 tablespoons olive oil
1 teaspoon oregano
1 teaspoon sage

2 dried red chilies
⅓ cup grated fresh gingerroot
Salt
Pepper

In a medium bowl, cover beans with water. Soak 8 to 10 hours. In a large saucepan, boil beans and water 10 minutes. Drain well. In a large saucepan, heat oil. Add beans, oregano, sage, chilies and ginger. Stir well. Cook 2 to 3 minutes. Add enough water to cover beans by 1½ inches. Cover and simmer 2 hours or until tender. Drain well. Remove chilies. Season with salt and pepper. Makes 4 servings.

Per serving: 225 kcal/12 g protein/9 g fat/26 g carbohydrate/14 g fiber

Mexican Beans $\boxed{V}$

1 cup dried red kidney beans
2 tablespoons olive oil
1 teaspoon oregano
3 garlic cloves, minced
2 dried red chilies

1 (14-oz.) can tomatoes
2 red bell peppers, cored, seeded, chopped
1 large onion, thinly sliced in rings

In a medium bowl, cover beans with water. Soak 8 to 10 hours. In a large saucepan, boil beans and liquid 10 minutes; discard liquid. In a large saucepan, heat 1 tablespoon of oil. Add beans, oregano, garlic and red chilies. Cook 1 to 2 minutes. Add tomatoes and enough water to cover beans by 1½ inches. Cover and simmer 1½ hours or until beans are tender. Drain well.

In a medium saucepan, cook peppers in remaining oil 5 minutes or until tender. Add red peppers and oil to beans. Stir in onion rings. Remove red chilies. Let stand, covered, 10 minutes. Makes 4 servings.

Per serving: 260 kcal/14 g protein/9 g fat/32 g carbohydrate/17 g fiber

Green Bean Stew   *Photograph, page 78*

¾ cup dried navy beans
1¼ cups celery stock (page 43)
2 bay leaves
½ lb. fresh green beans, trimmed, sliced
1 lb. fresh lima beans, shelled

⅔ cup pesto sauce
2 tablespoons butter or margarine
¼ cup all-purpose flour
7¼ cups low-fat milk
Salt
Pepper

In a small bowl, cover navy beans with water. Soak 2 hours; drain. In a large saucepan, simmer navy beans, celery stock and bay leaves 1 hour. In a large saucepan, cook green beans and lima beans in a small amount of water, covered, over low heat until just tender. Drain. Add green beans and lima beans to navy beans. Remove bay leaves. Mix in pesto sauce.

In a small saucepan, melt butter or margarine. Stir in flour to make a roux. Slowly add milk. Season with salt and pepper. Add sauce to beans. Stir well. Reheat. Makes 4 servings.

Per serving: 200 kcal/11 g protein/8 g fat/23 g carbohydrate/4 g fiber

Fasoulia

V

1 cup dried navy beans
3 tablespoons olive oil
10 garlic cloves, minced
½ teaspoon thyme
½ teaspoon sage
2 teaspoons oregano

2 bay leaves
Boiling water
2 tablespoons tomato purée
1 large onion, thinly sliced
Salt
Pepper

In a medium bowl, cover beans with water. Soak 8 to 10 hours. In a medium saucepan, boil beans and liquid 10 minutes; drain. In a large saucepan, heat oil. Add beans, garlic and herbs. Stir well. Add enough boiling water to cover beans by 1 inch. Stir in tomato purée. Cook over a very low heat, covered, 3 hours or until beans are tender. Add onion. Season with salt and pepper. Let stand, covered, 10 minutes. Remove bay leaves. Makes 4 servings.

Per serving: 270 kcal/13 g protein/12 g fat/30 g carbohydrate/15 g fiber

Garbanzo Beans & Spinach

V

¾ cup dried garbanzo beans
1 lb. potatoes, quartered
2 tablespoons butter or
  margarine
2 tablespoons olive oil
1 lb. fresh leaf spinach, trimmed,
  chopped

3 garlic cloves, minced
1¼ cups dry cider
3 tablespoons fresh mint, finely
  chopped
Salt
Pepper

In a medium bowl, cover beans with water. Soak 8 to 10 hours. In a large saucepan, cook beans in boiling water 2 hours. Drain well. In a large saucepan, cook potatoes in lightly salted water until tender. Drain. Add potatoes to beans. Set aside. In a medium saucepan, heat butter or margarine and oil. Add spinach and garlic. Cook over low heat 10 minutes. Set aside. Add cider to beans and potatoes. Boil 2 minutes. Stir spinach into beans and potatoes. Add mint. Season with salt and pepper. Makes 4 servings.

Per serving: 400 kcal/17 g protein/16 g fat/50 g carbohydrate/16 g fiber

Kosheri |V|

2 lbs. tomatoes
Salt
Pepper
2 onions, sliced in rings
⅔ cup low-fat milk or
  unsweetened soy milk
½ cup all-purpose flour
¼ cup corn oil
2½ cups cooked long-grain rice
1½ cups cooked green lentils
1½ cups cooked whole-wheat
  macaroni

Hot Sauce:
1 teaspoon cumin
1 teaspoon coriander
½ teaspoon chili powder
½ teaspoon celery salt
4 tablespoons tomato purée
¾ cup vegetable stock (page 43),
  heated

In a large saucepan, cook tomatoes over medium heat 10 to 15 minutes or until tomatoes are reduced to a pulp. Strain through a sieve. Season with salt and pepper. Set aside. In a medium bowl, soak onions in milk 1 to 2 minutes; drain. Place flour in a paper bag. Shake onions in flour until all are evenly covered. In a medium skillet, heat oil. Add onions. Fry until crisp. Drain on paper towels. Set aside.

To assemble kosheri, spoon rice on a large serving platter. Pour ⅓ of tomato sauce over rice. Spoon lentils in center of rice. Spoon macaroni in center of lentils. Pour remaining tomato sauce over lentils and macaroni. Garnish with onions. Serve with Hot Sauce. Makes 4 servings.

Hot Sauce
In a small bowl, mix spices and tomato purée. Add vegetable stock. Stir to make a paste.

Per serving: 470 kcal/19 g protein/6 g fat/90 g carbohydrate/12 g fiber

Kosheri
OVERLEAF: Green Bean Stew (*left*, page 74), Indian Rice (*center*, page 92), Buckwheat Noodles with Mushroom Sauce (*right*, page 85)

Green Lentil Dhal $\boxed{V}$

1 cup dried green lentils
2 tablespoons corn oil
⅓ cup grated fresh gingerroot
3 garlic cloves, minced
1 teaspoon cumin
1 teaspoon coriander

1½ teaspoons turmeric
1 tablespoon garam masala or
    curry powder
Boiling water
Salt
Pepper

In a medium bowl, cover lentils with water. Soak 30 minutes; drain. In a large saucepan, heat oil. Add ginger, garlic and spices. Cook 1 to 2 minutes. Add lentils. Add enough boiling water to cover lentils by 1 inch. Cook over low heat 30 minutes. Stir occasionally. Season with salt and pepper.

    If desired, in a blender, process lentils to a purée. Makes 4 servings.

Per serving: 240 kcal/14 g protein/8 g fat/30 g carbohydrate/7 g fiber

Millet & Bean Croquettes

½ cup dried split mung beans
2 tablespoons olive oil
⅔ cup millet
2 onions, finely chopped
1 teaspoon oregano
1 teaspoon sage
3 garlic cloves, minced
2 tablespoons shoyu soy sauce

1 egg, beaten
3 tablespoons fresh parsley,
    chopped
Salt
Pepper
1 tablespoon whole-wheat flour
Oil

In a small bowl, cover beans with water. Soak 2 hours. In a medium saucepan, bring beans to a boil. Reduce heat. Simmer 20 minutes. Drain well. Mash to a rough purée. Set aside. In a medium saucepan, heat 1 tablespoon oil. Add millet. Cook 2 to 3 minutes or until brown. Cover millet with boiling water. Simmer 20 minutes. Remove from heat. Set aside. In a medium skillet, heat remaining 1 tablespoon oil. Cook onions, oregano, sage and garlic until onions are soft.

    Drain millet. Add millet to beans. Mix in onions and herbs. Add shoyu soy sauce, egg and parsley. Season with salt and pepper. Mix thoroughly. Stir in flour. In a large skillet, heat oil. Drop tablespoons of mixture into hot oil. Cook each side until brown and crisp. Drain on paper towels. Makes 4 servings.

Per serving: 270 kcal/12 g protein/10 g fat/35 g carbohydrate/9 g fiber

---

Millet & Bean Croquettes (*above*), Polenta (page 84)

Khichhari

$\boxed{V}$

½ cup dried brown lentils
½ cup dried split green peas
¼ cup corn oil
2 onions, sliced
⅓ cup grated fresh gingerroot
½ teaspoon crushed cinnamon
   bark
½ teaspoon cardamom
½ teaspoon nutmeg
½ teaspoon mace

½ teaspoon cumin
½ teaspoon coriander
½ teaspoon mustard seed
1 tablespoon raisins
1 tablespoon almonds
1 tablespoon cashew nuts
¾ cup long-grain rice
5 cups boiling water
Salt
Pepper

In a small bowl, cover lentils and peas with water. Soak 30 minutes. Drain well. Preheat oven to 350F (175C).

In a large saucepan, heat oil. Add onions, ginger and all spices. Sauté 1 to 2 minutes. Add raisins and nuts. Cook until brown. Stir in lentils, split peas and rice. Add water; mix well. Pour mixture into an 11" × 7" baking dish. Bake in preheated oven, tightly covered, 30 to 40 minutes. Season with salt and pepper. Makes 4 servings.

Per serving: 520 kcal/18 g protein/19 g fat/75 g carbohydrate/10 g fiber

Millet Pilav

2 tablespoons olive oil
2 red bell peppers, cored, seeded,
   chopped
1 onion, chopped
2 zucchini, chopped
3 garlic cloves, minced
1⅓ cups millet
1¼ cups vegetable stock
   (page 43)

½ cup grated Parmesan cheese
⅓ cup shredded Gruyère cheese
3 tablespoons fresh parsley, finely
   chopped
Salt
Pepper

In a large saucepan, heat oil. Add peppers, onion, zucchini and garlic. Cook 1 to 2 minutes. Add millet; cook until millet is brown. Add vegetable stock. Simmer over very low heat, tightly covered, 20 minutes. Stir in Parmesan cheese, Gruyère cheese and parsley. Season with salt and pepper. Makes 4 servings.

Per serving: 370 kcal/13 g protein/16 g fat/46 g carbohydrate/4 g fiber

Hot Tabouleh

3 tablespoons olive oil
1¼ cups buckwheat groats
5 garlic cloves, minced
Grated peel and juice of 2
  lemons
3¾ cups vegetable stock
  (page 43)

1 bunch fresh parsley, finely
  chopped
1 bunch green onions, chopped
Salt
Pepper

In a large saucepan, heat oil. Add buckwheat groats and garlic. Stir well.
Cook 1 to 2 minutes. Add lemon peel and juice and vegetable stock. Bring
to a boil. Reduce heat. Simmer 10 minutes. Let stand, covered, 10 minutes.
Drain. Add parsley and onions. Season with salt and pepper. Makes 4
servings.

Per serving: 260 kcal/ 5 g protein/ 13 g fat/ 33 g carbohydrate/ 4 g fiber

Buckwheat Rissoles

1 cup buckwheat groats
3 garlic cloves, minced
3 tablespoons tomato purée
1 teaspoon ground cumin
1 teaspoon coriander
1 tablespoon garam masala or
  curry powder
1 egg, beaten

3 tablespoons fresh parsley,
  chopped
3 tablespoons fresh chives,
  chopped
Salt
Pepper
2 tablespoons corn oil

In a medium bowl, cover buckwheat groats with boiling water. Let stand
20 minutes. Drain thoroughly. Add garlic, tomato purée, spices, egg,
parsley and chives. Season with salt and pepper. Stir well. In a medium
skillet, heat oil. Form mixture into small cakes. Fry until brown and crisp.
Drain on paper towels. Makes 4 servings.

Per serving: 240 kcal/ 7 g protein/ 10 g fat/ 33 g carbohydrate/ 4 g fiber

Polenta

Photograph, page 80

5 cups water
1½ cups cornmeal
1 teaspoon sea salt

1 egg, beaten
Cornmeal
Corn oil

Grease a large shallow baking dish. In a large saucepan, bring water to a boil. Pour cornmeal into water in a slow, steady stream, stirring continually. Add salt. Reduce heat. Cook, covered, 15 minutes. Stir occasionally. Pour polenta into prepared dish. Let stand 8 to 10 hours.

Cut polenta in 3″ × 2″ pieces. Dip into beaten egg. Roll in cornmeal to coat evenly. In a medium skillet, heat oil. Fry polenta until brown. Drain on paper towels. Makes 12 sticks.

Per stick: 95 kcal/1 g protein/3 g fat/17 g carbohydrate/1 g fiber

Barley & Corn

2 tablespoons olive oil
1 cup pearl barley
3¾ cups vegetable stock
　(page 43)

1 (12-oz.) can whole kernel corn
⅔ cup low-fat plain yogurt
Salt
Pepper

In a large saucepan, heat oil. Add barley. Sauté 2 to 3 minutes. Add vegetable stock; bring to a boil. Simmer 50 minutes or until barley is cooked. Drain; cool. Add corn to barley. Mix in yogurt. Stir well. Season with salt and pepper. Makes 4 servings.

Per serving: 290 kcal/6 g protein/9 g fat/ 50 g carbohydrate/4 g fiber

PASTA, RICE & PIZZA

Excellent whole-wheat pasta is now available in supermarkets as well as smaller delicatessens. The best health food stores have been selling it for years in a variety of shapes and sizes. Gourmets of Italian food shudder at the thought, believing that it will make traditional dishes too heavy. This is not so – whole-wheat pasta gives greater flavor to a dish. It is easier to time while cooking so that the pasta is firm to the bite.

Buckwheat noodles come from Japan and have plenty of flavor. Simple to cook, they are blanched in boiling water and left for eight minutes.

Some of the best traditional Italian dishes are the simplest. *Spaghetti all' aglio* can be ordered in any tiny restaurant all over Sicily. It is simply several cloves of garlic minced and sprinkled over the spaghetti with a little olive oil or butter. Washed down with a glass of red wine, it is a perfect lunch.

There are no brown rice recipes in this book. However, for readers who enjoy the virtues of brown rice, the recipes can be adapted. Brown rice needs 45 to 50 minutes' cooking time.

Italian purists have also complained over the years that risottos must be cooked on top of the range and not in the oven. However, when the oven method is used, rice never sticks to the bottom of the pan.

Buckwheat Noodles with Mushroom Sauce
Photograph, page 79

12 oz. buckwheat noodles

Mushroom Sauce:
2 tablespoons butter or
   margarine

½ lb. fresh mushrooms, finely
   chopped
Salt
Pepper
⅔ cup low-fat plain yogurt
1 tablespoon shoyu soy sauce

In a large saucepan, pour boiling water over noodles. Cover; let stand 8 minutes. Drain.

Mushroom Sauce
In a medium skillet, melt butter or margarine. Add mushrooms. Sauté 5 minutes. Season with salt and pepper. Stir in yogurt and shoyu soy sauce.

To serve, pour sauce over noodles. Makes 4 servings.

Per serving: 360 kcal/12 g protein/8 g fat/65 g carbohydrate/7 g fiber

Fettucine with Vegetables

Photograph on cover

8 oz. fettucine noodles
¼ cup butter or margarine
1 zucchini, cut in julienne strips
1 carrot, cut in julienne strips
¼ cup sliced mushrooms
¼ cup sliced green onion

½ teaspoon basil
½ cup thawed frozen peas
Salt
Pepper
⅓ cup grated Parmesan cheese
Fresh celery leaf, if desired

In a large saucepan, cook noodles in boiling salted water until tender but firm. Drain well. Set aside. In a medium skillet, melt butter or margarine. Sauté zucchini and carrot until nearly tender. Stir in mushrooms, green onion and basil. Cook 2 minutes. Stir in green peas. Combine vegetable mixture with noodles. Season with salt and pepper. Sprinkle Parmesan cheese over top. Garnish with celery leaf, if desired. Makes 4 servings.

Per serving: 295 kcal/9 g protein/8 g fat/30 g carbohydrate/2 g fiber

Tagliatelle with Eggs & Herbs

Photograph, page 89

12 oz. whole-wheat tagliatelle
   noodles
2 tablespoons butter or
   margarine
1 bunch fresh parsley, finely
   chopped

1 bunch fresh basil, finely
   chopped
2 eggs, beaten
Salt
Pepper

In a large saucepan, cook noodles in boiling salted water 5 minutes or until tender but firm. Drain well. In a large skillet, melt butter or margarine. Add parsley, basil and eggs. Season with salt and pepper. Before eggs have set, pour noodles in skillet. Shake skillet so eggs and herbs cook onto noodles. Makes 4 servings.

Per serving: 360 kcal/15 g protein/10g fat/56 g carbohydrate/9 g fiber

Macaroni & Cheese

1¼ cups skim milk
3 bay leaves
10 oz. whole-wheat macaroni
½ cup shredded Cheddar cheese
⅛ teaspoon sage
⅔ cup grated Parmesan cheese
½ cup shredded Gruyère cheese

2 tablespoons butter or
   margarine
¼ cup all-purpose flour
Salt
Pepper
1 bunch fresh parsley, finely
   chopped

Preheat oven to 400F (200C). Grease a 13" × 9" baking dish.

In a small saucepan, heat milk and bay leaves. Remove from heat. Let stand. In a large saucepan, cook macaroni in boiling salted water 5 minutes or until tender but firm. Drain well.

In prepared baking dish, layer ⅓ of macaroni. Sprinkle with Cheddar cheese and sage. Layer another ⅓ of macaroni in baking dish. Sprinkle with Parmesan cheese. Add remaining macaroni. Sprinkle with Gruyère cheese.

In a small saucepan, melt butter or margarine. Stir in flour to make a roux. Remove bay leaves from milk. Pour milk into roux, stirring continuously. Season with salt and pepper. Stir in parsley. Pour over macaroni. Bake in preheated oven 25 to 30 minutes. Makes 4 servings.

Per serving: 495 kcal/25 g protein/21 g fat/55 g carbohydrate/7 g fiber

Cannelloni with Walnut Cheese*

¾ lb. whole-wheat cannelloni
   noodles
1 bunch green onions, chopped
¾ cup chopped walnuts
1 cup cottage cheese
⅔ cup grated Parmesan cheese
1 cup whole-wheat breadcrumbs

2 tablespoons butter or
   margarine
¼ cup all-purpose flour
1¼ cups skim milk
⅓ cup shredded Gruyère cheese
Salt
Pepper

Preheat oven to 350F (175C). Grease a 13" × 9" baking dish.

In a large saucepan, cook noodles in boiling water 10 minutes or until tender but firm. Drain well.

To make stuffing, in a medium bowl, mix green onions, walnuts, cottage cheese and Parmesan cheese. Add breadcrumbs; mix thoroughly. To make sauce, in a small saucepan, melt butter or margarine. Stir in flour to make a roux. Gradually add milk, stirring continuously. Add Gruyère cheese. Season with salt and pepper.

To assemble, spoon a small amount of stuffing into each noodle. Arrange in prepared baking dish. Pour sauce over each cannelloni. Bake in preheated oven 15 minutes. Makes 4 servings.

Per serving: 390 kcal/22 g protein/25 g fat/21 g carbohydrate/3 g fiber

Lasagne Verdi

10 whole-wheat lasagne noodles
2 lbs. zucchini, sliced
2 lbs. fresh spinach, trimmed
1 cup shredded Cheddar cheese
2 lbs. fresh green peas, shelled
1¼ cups low-fat milk
2 eggs, beaten
⅛ teaspoon sage
Salt

Pepper
2 tablespoons butter or
   margarine
½ cup all-purpose flour
1¼ cups low-fat milk
¾ cup shredded Cheddar cheese
Salt
Pepper

Preheat oven to 400F (200C). Grease a 13″ × 9″ baking dish.

In a large saucepan, cook noodles in boiling salted water 10 to 15 minutes. Drain separately on paper towels. Lay ⅔ of noodles on bottom and sides of prepared baking dish.

In a large saucepan, cook zucchini and spinach 10 to 12 minutes. Using a wooden spoon, chop spinach. Arrange spinach and zucchini over noodles in baking dish. Sprinkle Cheddar cheese over spinach and zucchini. In a medium saucepan, cook peas in boiling water 8 minutes; drain. In a blender, process peas, milk, eggs and sage to a purée. Season with salt and pepper. Pour pea purée over cheese. Cover with remaining noodles.

To make sauce, in a medium saucepan, melt butter or margarine. Stir in flour to make a roux. Gradually add milk, stirring continuously. Add Cheddar cheese. Season with salt and pepper. Pour sauce over lasagne, covering completely. Bake in preheated oven 30 minutes, or until top is brown and interior is bubbling. Makes 6 servings.

Per serving: 480 kcal/34 g protein/19 g fat/47 g carbohydrate/22 g fiber

French Gnocchi

1¼ cups water
2 tablespoons butter or
  margarine
1 teaspoon sea salt
½ teaspoon pepper
½ teaspoon grated nutmeg
¾ cup all-purpose flour

4 eggs
½ cup grated Parmesan cheese
⅓ cup shredded Gruyère cheese
2 cups cooked mashed potatoes
1 recipe Hot Sauce, Kosheri (omit
  cumin and chili powder,
  page 76)

In a medium saucepan, bring water to a boil. Stir in butter or margarine, salt, pepper and nutmeg. Add flour. Remove from heat. Beat mixture until flour and water combine. Return to heat. Stir vigorously until paste begins to leave sides of pan. Remove from heat. Beat in eggs, one by one to make a *pâte à choux*. In a medium bowl, mix Parmesan cheese, Gruyère cheese and potatoes. Beat potato mixture into *pâte à choux*. On a floured surface, roll out spoonfuls of mixture.

In a large saucepan, bring salted water to a boil. Reduce heat; simmer. Poach gnocchi 15 minutes or until doubled in size. Drain well. Make Hot Sauce as directed. Serve French Gnocchi with Hot Sauce. Makes 4 servings.

Per serving: 400 kcal/17 g protein/18 g fat/45 g carbohydrate/2 g fiber

Variation
Herb Gnocchi: Add 2 tablespoons finely chopped parsley and 2 tablespoons finely chopped mint when potato mixture is beaten into *pâte à choux*. Serve with melted butter or margarine.

Per serving: 440 kcal/17 g protein/23 g fat/45 g carbohydrate/2 g fiber

Variation
Gnocchi Baked with Cheese: Preheat oven to 400F (200C).
Make 1 recipe French Gnocchi. When gnocchi have been poached and drained, arrange in a greased large shallow baking dish. Cover with 2 ounces mozzarella cheese, thinly sliced. Bake in preheated oven 10 minutes.

Per serving: 445 kcal/20 g protein/22 g fat/45 g carbohydrate/2 g fiber

Riso Verdi (*above*, page 93), French Gnocchi

Indian Rice

Photograph, page 78

1½ cups long-grain rice
4 cups water
⅛ teaspoon saffron
2 tablespoons corn oil
2 onions, finely sliced
3 garlic cloves, minced
⅓ cup grated fresh gingerroot
1 teaspoon cumin
1 teaspoon fennel
1 teaspoon fenugreek

1 teaspoon poppy seeds
1 tablespoon chopped cashew
   nuts
1 tablespoon chopped almonds
1 tablespoon golden raisins
Salt
Pepper
3 tablespoons chopped fresh
   cilantro

In a large saucepan, boil rice, water and saffron 15 minutes or until rice is just tender. Drain well. In a medium saucepan, heat oil. Add onions, garlic and ginger. Cook 5 minutes. Add spices, nuts and raisins. Cook 1 to 2 minutes. Season with salt and pepper. Stir nut and spice mixture and cilantro into rice. Makes 4 servings.

Per serving: 445 kcal/8 g protein/14 g fat/79 g carbohydrate/4 g fiber

Stuffed Pancakes

¾ cup whole-wheat flour
½ teaspoon salt
2 eggs
1 tablespoon olive oil
⅔ cup milk
½ cup water
1 recipe Hot Sauce, Kosheri (omit
   cumin and chili powder,
   page 76)

¾ cup ricotta cheese
½ cup Roquefort cheese
1 bunch green onions, chopped
1 bunch fresh parsley, chopped
1 egg
Salt
Pepper

To make batter, in a medium bowl, sift flour and salt. Make a well in center. Break eggs in well. Mix eggs and flour together to a smooth paste. Add oil, milk and water. Whisk batter. Let stand 1 to 2 hours.

Make Hot Sauce as directed. Preheat oven to 400F (200C). Grease a 13″ × 9″ baking dish.

To make stuffing, in a medium bowl, mix ricotta cheese, Roquefort cheese, green onions, parsley and egg. Season with salt and pepper.

Beat pancake batter. Using a greased griddle, make 8 (7-inch) pancakes. Place on paper towels. Fill each pancake with ⅛ of stuffing. Fold like an envelope. Arrange pancakes in prepared baking dish. Pour Hot Sauce over each pancake. Bake in preheated oven 10 minutes. Makes 8 servings.

Per serving: 1550 kcal/64 g protein/101 g fat/103 g carbohydrate/10 g fiber

Riso Verdi

Photograph, page 90

5 cups cooked long-grain rice
1 lb. fresh green peas, shelled
1 lb. fresh snow peas, sliced
2 tablespoons butter or
    margarine
1 bunch fresh parsley, finely
    chopped

½ cup shelled pistachio nuts
3 tablespoons dry vermouth
Salt
Pepper

Preheat oven to 300F (150C).

On a baking sheet, bake rice in preheated oven 10 minutes or until dry. In a large saucepan, cook green peas and snow peas in a small amount of water until tender. Drain well. In a large bowl, mix green peas, snow peas, butter or margarine, parsley and pistachio nuts. Stir rice into pea mixture. Mix well. Pour vermouth over rice. Season with salt and pepper. Bake in preheated oven 2 to 3 minutes. Makes 4 servings.

Per serving: 490 kcal/15 g protein/14 g fat/77 g carbohydrate/13 g fiber

Beets & Ginger Rice

1 lb. raw beets, peeled, coarsely
    chopped
1 small cabbage, chopped
⅓ cup chopped fresh gingerroot
Boiling water

1 teaspoon salt
¾ cup long-grain rice
2 tablespoons butter or
    margarine
2 beets, peeled, grated

Preheat oven to 325F (150C).

In a 13" × 9" baking dish, combine chopped beets, cabbage and ginger. Cover vegetables with boiling water. Add salt. Bake in preheated oven 3 to 4 hours.

Remove from oven. Drain liquid from vegetables. Reserve liquid; discard vegetables. In a medium saucepan, cook rice in reserved liquid until rice absorbs all liquid. Stir in butter or margarine. Add grated beets. Makes 4 servings.

Per serving: 295 kcal/9 g protein/6 g fat/55 g carbohydrate/9 g fiber

Vegetable Risotto

1 tablespoon olive oil
2 zucchini, chopped
2 onions, sliced
1 lb. fresh mushrooms, sliced
5 garlic cloves, minced
1¼ cups long-grain rice
⅔ cup dry red wine
1 (14-oz.) can tomatoes
1 tablespoon tomato purée

Salt
Pepper
Water
3 tablespoons fresh parsley,
   finely chopped
⅔ cup grated Parmesan cheese
2 tablespoons butter or
   margarine

Preheat oven to 350F (175C).

In a large saucepan, heat oil. Add zucchini, onions, mushrooms and garlic. Sauté 1 to 2 minutes. Add rice. Cook 1 to 2 minutes, stirring continuously. Add wine, tomatoes and tomato purée. Season with salt and pepper. Pour into a 13″ × 9″ baking dish. Cover rice with water. Bake in preheated oven 30 to 40 minutes. Stir in parsley, Parmesan cheese and butter or margarine. Makes 4 servings.

Per serving: 445 kcal/14 g protein/14 g fat/70 g carbohydrate/8 g fiber

Variation
Suppli: Mix 2 tablespoons of a finely chopped fresh herb – parsley, mint, basil – into cold risotto. Form small croquettes, placing slices of mozzarella cheese inside croquettes. Dip into beaten egg; roll in fine whole-wheat breadcrumbs. Fry in hot olive oil.

Pizza

Dough:

1¾ cups all-purpose flour
½ teaspoon salt
2 (¼-oz.) pkgs. active dry yeast
2 tablespoons milk, warmed
1 egg, beaten
2 tablespoons olive oil
2 to 3 tablespoons warm water

Filling:

2 tablespoons olive oil
2 onions, sliced
1 green bell pepper, sliced
5 garlic cloves, minced
1 teaspoon oregano
1 (14-oz.) can tomatoes
2 tablespoons tomato purée
Salt
Pepper
5 tomatoes, sliced
12 black olives, pitted, sliced
2 tablespoons capers

Dough

In a large bowl, sift flour and salt. In a small bowl, mix yeast and milk. Let stand 10 minutes or until frothy. Add yeast to flour. Stir in egg, oil and water. Knead dough until smooth and elastic. Form into a ball. Let stand, covered, in a warm place 2 hours or until dough rises.

Preheat oven to 425F (218C). Grease a baking sheet.

Smooth dough on baking sheet, pressing and pulling dough. Make a small ridge of dough around edge of baking sheet. Let stand 10 minutes.

To make filling, in a medium saucepan, heat oil. Add onions, pepper, garlic and oregano. Cook over low heat 10 minutes. Add tomatoes. Simmer 45 minutes. Add tomato purée. Season with salt and pepper. Cook 5 minutes.

Spoon filling over dough. Top with tomato slices, olives and capers. Let stand 10 minutes. Bake in preheated oven 15 minutes. Adjust oven to 350F (175C). Bake 15 minutes. Makes 4 servings.

Per serving: 415 kcal/10 g protein/18 g fat/57 g carbohydrate/5 g fiber

Tomato & Chili Pizza

1 recipe Dough, Pizza (see
   page 95)
1 tablespoon olive oil
2 onions, finely chopped
3 garlic cloves, minced
2 tablespoons dried oregano

1 (1-lb. 12-oz.) can tomatoes
3 dried red chilies
Salt
Pepper
3 tablespoons tomato purée
4 oz. mozzarella cheese, sliced

Make dough as directed. Preheat oven to 425F (218C). Grease a baking sheet.

In a large saucepan, heat oil. Add onions, garlic and oregano. Reduce heat. Cook 5 minutes. Stir in tomatoes and chilies. Cook 30 minutes. Season with salt and pepper. Add tomato purée. Cook 5 minutes. Remove and discard chilies. Spread filling over prepared dough. Let stand 10 minutes. Bake in preheated oven 15 minutes. Top with mozzarella cheese. Adjust oven to 350F (175C). Bake 15 minutes. Makes 4 servings.

Per serving: 490 kcal/19 g protein/23 g fat/55 g carbohydrate/5 g fiber

Mushroom & Artichoke Pizza

1 recipe Dough, Pizza (page 95)
1 tablespoon olive oil
1 teaspoon dried oregano
3 garlic cloves, minced
2 onions, sliced
¾ lb. fresh mushrooms, sliced

4 tablespoons tomato purée
Salt
Pepper
3 to 4 canned artichoke hearts,
   sliced
4 oz. mozzarella cheese, sliced

Make dough as directed. Preheat oven to 425F (218C). Grease a baking sheet.

In a medium saucepan, heat oil. Add oregano, garlic, onions and mushrooms. Cook over low heat 10 minutes. Add tomato purée. Season with salt and pepper. Spread filling over prepared dough. Arrange artichoke hearts over pizza. Let stand 10 minutes. Bake in preheated oven 15 minutes. Top with mozzarella cheese. Adjust oven to 350F (175C). Bake 15 minutes. Makes 4 servings.

Per serving: 480 kcal/19 g protein/15 g fat/52 g carbohydrate/6 g fiber

VEGETABLE DISHES

One of the great charms of vegetarian cooking is that no food, dish or meal is confined within a straight jacket. Some of the following recipes could be a main course, for example the Stuffed Cabbage (page 103), yet served to a larger group it would make an excellent beginning to a meal. Other recipes are side dishes, but would make equally delicious light suppers or lunches, like the Potato and Pepper Gratin (page 105).

Vegetarian food need never be bland. To get the full flavor from spices, make sure they are fresh. Always throw away any spices that have been kept longer than a few months. Keep spices away from the light and make sure they are tightly closed. Try to use herbs straight from the garden. Cook dishes seasonally, ensuring that you get the best from fresh vegetables. Most of us are lucky now and can also cook with the many types of imported vegetables. Avoid buying those that seem limp or bruised – the flavor is generally feeble (apart from the vitamins being lost).

Artichoke Stew $\boxed{\text{V}}$

12 baby artichokes, trimmed
6¼ cups water
2 green bell peppers, cored, seeded
1 lb. baby carrots, thinly sliced
1 lb. fresh green peas, shelled
2 tablespoons butter or margarine
¼ cup all-purpose flour
Salt
Pepper

Discard tough outer leaves of artichokes. In a large saucepan, boil artichokes and water 5 minutes. Add peppers and carrots to artichokes. Simmer 15 minutes. Add peas. Cook 10 minutes. Drain. Reserve liquid.

In a small saucepan, melt butter or margarine. Stir in flour to make a roux. Add enough reserved liquid to roux to make a thin sauce. Season with salt and pepper. Pour over vegetables. Reheat over low heat. Makes 4 servings.

Per serving: 190 kcal/10 g protein/6 g fat/26 g carbohydrate/10 g fiber

Artichoke Soufflé

4 large artichokes	1¼ cups skim milk
5 eggs, separated	Salt
½ cup shredded Gruyère cheese	Pepper

In a large saucepan, cover artichokes with water. Boil 45 minutes. Drain; cool. Scrape flesh from bottom of each artichoke leaf. Using a sharp knife, remove hairy choke from each artichoke; discard. Dice pad of flesh at bottom of artichoke.

Preheat oven to 400F (200C). Grease a soufflé dish.

In a blender, process artichoke flesh, egg yolks, Gruyère cheese and milk to a purée. Whip egg whites until stiff. Fold egg whites into artichoke purée. Gently pour into prepared soufflé dish.

Bake 20 minutes or until top is well risen and brown. Serve immediately. Center and bottom of soufflé will be liquid. Makes 4 servings.

Per serving: 230 kcal/17 g protein/15 g fat/8 g carbohydrate/10 g fiber

Baked Parsnips with Pine Nuts

Photograph, page 100

1½ lbs. parsnips, peeled, chopped	Salt
2 tablespoons butter or	Pepper
margarine	¼ cup pine nuts, roasted

Preheat oven to 400F (200C). Grease an 11" × 7" baking dish.

In a large saucepan, boil parsnips in salted water 10 minutes ot until soft. Drain well. In a blender, process parsnips and butter or margarine to a purée. Season with salt and pepper. Pour into prepared baking dish. Sprinkle pine nuts over top. Bake in preheated oven 5 minutes. Makes 4 servings.

Per serving: 170 kcal/4 g protein/9 g fat/20 g carbohydrate/7 g fiber

---

Artichoke Soufflé
OVERLEAF: Baked Parsnips with Pine Nuts (*left*), Leek Timbale (*center*, page 106), Broccoli with Maltese Sauce (*right*, page 104)

Stuffed Cabbage

12 large Savoy cabbage leaves	1 cup whole-wheat breadcrumbs
2 tablespoons olive oil	½ cup chopped walnuts
2 green bell peppers, sliced	Salt
2 onions, sliced	Pepper
1 teaspoon oregano	2¼ cups vegetable stock
1 teaspoon dill weed	(page 43)
¾ cup ricotta cheese	

Remove roughest part at bottom of cabbage leaves. In a large saucepan, blanch cabbage leaves in boiling water. Drain well. In a large skillet, heat oil. Add peppers, onions, oregano and dill weed. Cook until vegetables are soft. In a large bowl, combined cooked vegetables, ricotta cheese, breadcrumbs and walnuts. Season with salt and pepper.

Place a small amount of stuffing on each cabbage leaf. Roll up, tucking in corners. In a large saucepan, arrange stuffed cabbage, packing tightly. Pour vegetable stock over stuffed cabbage. Bring to a boil. Reduce heat. Simmer 20 minutes. Drain well. Makes 4 servings.

Per leaf: 125 kcal/4 g protein/9 g fat/8 g carbohydrate/3 g fiber

Stuffed Peppers

4 large green bell peppers	3 tablespoons chopped fresh
1½ cups whole-wheat	parsley
bread crumbs	Dash hot-pepper sauce
2 large onions, finely chopped	1 cup ricotta cheese
3 garlic cloves, minced	2 eggs
10 black olives, pitted, chopped	Salt
2 tablespoons capers	Pepper

Preheat oven to 350F (175C).

Cut tops off peppers; reserve. Core and seed peppers; set aside. To make stuffing, in a large bowl, mix bread crumbs, onions, garlic, olives, capers, parsley, hot-pepper sauce, ricotta cheese and eggs. Season with salt and pepper. Fill peppers with stuffing.

Stand peppers upright in a 9-inch-square baking dish, packing tight. Pour 1-inch water in baking dish around peppers. Place reserved tops on stuffed peppers. Bake in preheated oven, covered, 40 minutes. Makes 4 servings.

Per serving: 305 kcal/13 g protein/19 g fat/22 g carbohydrate/5 g fiber

Stuffed Pepper, Stuffed Cabbage

Broccoli with Maltese Sauce

Photograph, page 101

2½ lbs. fresh broccoli, trimmed
Grated peel and juice of 2
　oranges
½ cup butter or margarine

⅛ teaspoon cayenne pepper
Salt
Pepper
3 egg yolks

In a large saucepan, steam broccoli 5 to 6 minutes or until tender. In a small saucepan, cook orange peel and juice, butter or margarine and cayenne pepper until butter or margarine melts. Season with salt and pepper.

In a blender, process egg yolks very slowly while pouring butter and orange mixture into egg yolks. Blend well. Pour over broccoli. Makes 6 servings.

Per serving: 250 kcal/9 g protein/20 g fat/9 g carbohydrate/8 g fiber

Stuffed Eggplant ⬚V⬚

2 eggplants, halved
2 tablespoons olive oil
2 onions, sliced
2 zucchini, sliced
3 garlic cloves, minced
½ teaspoon paprika
½ teaspoon ginger
½ teaspoon cumin
½ teaspoon garam masala or
　curry powder

⅓ cup cooked mashed potatoes
2 tomatoes, peeled, diced
1 tablespoon tomato purée
Salt
Pepper
2 tablespoons finely chopped
　cilantro

Preheat oven to 375F (190C). Grease a 13″ × 9″ baking dish.

In a large saucepan, cover eggplants with water. Boil 5 minutes. Drain well. Scoop out center flesh, leaving ¼-inch shell. In a large skillet, heat oil. Add onions, zucchini, garlic and spices. Sauté 5 minutes or until vegetables are soft. Stir in eggplant flesh, potatoes, tomatoes and tomato purée. Season with salt and pepper. Cook 1 to 2 minutes.

Spoon stuffing into eggplant shells. Arrange in prepared baking dish. Bake 20 minutes. Sprinkle cilantro over top. Makes 4 servings.

Per serving: 135 kcal/3 g protein/8 g fat/14 g carbohydrate/5 g fiber

Potato & Pepper Gratin

1½ lbs. potatoes, peeled
2 tablespoons butter or
    margarine
3 tablespoons olive oil
4 green bell peppers, cored, seeded,
    sliced

1 onion, sliced
3 garlic cloves, minced
Salt
Pepper
⅓ cup grated Parmesan cheese

Preheat oven to 350F (175C). Grease a 13" × 9" baking dish.
　In a large saucepan, cover potatoes with water. Boil 15 minutes. Drain
well; slice. Set aside. In a large saucepan, heat butter or margarine and oil.
Add potatoes, peppers, onions and garlic. Season with salt and pepper.
Cook 5 minutes. Spoon into prepared baking dish. Sprinkle Parmesan
cheese over top. Bake in preheated oven 10 minutes. Makes 4 servings.

Per serving: 305 kcal/8 g protein/14 g fat/40 g carbohydrate/5 g fiber

Baked Fennel ⬚V

4 fennel roots, trimmed, halved
⅔ cup grated Parmesan cheese

Freshly ground black pepper
Butter or margarine

Preheat oven to 350F (175C). Grease a 13" × 9" baking dish.
　In a large saucepan, boil fennel in lightly salted water 10 minutes. Drain
well. Arrange fennel in prepared baking dish. Sprinkle Parmesan cheese
over fennel. Season with pepper. Dot with butter or margarine. Bake 10
minutes. Makes 4 servings.

Per serving: 155 kcal/9 g protein/12 g fat/3 g carbohydrate/4 g fiber

Potato Tarkari ⬚V

1½ lbs. potatoes
3 tablespoons corn oil
2 onions, sliced
⅓ cup grated fresh gingerroot
2 tablespoons green peppercorns
½ teaspoon paprika

½ teaspoon fenugreek
½ teaspoon mustard seeds
Salt
Pepper
2 tablespoons chopped cilantro

In a large saucepan, cover potatoes with water. Drain well; dice. Set aside.
In a large saucepan, heat oil. Add onions, ginger, peppercorns and spices.
Cook 1 to 2 minutes. Add potatoes. Season with salt and pepper. Cook,
covered, 10 minutes. Remove cover. Increase heat and brown potatoes.
Sprinkle cilantro over top. Makes 4 servings.

Per serving: 250 kcal/4 g protein/11 g fat/37 g carbohydrate/3 g fiber

Potato & Spinach Pie

1½ lbs. potatoes, peeled, sliced	Salt
2 tablespooons butter or	Pepper
margarine	1 egg
1½ lbs. fresh spinach, trimmed	1¼ cups skim milk
⅛ teaspoon grated nutmeg	

In a large bowl, soak potatoes in cold water 30 minutes. Rinse; drain well.
Preheat oven to 325F (150C). Grease a 3-inch deep pie dish.
In a large saucepan, melt butter or margarine. Add spinach. Cook,
covered, 10 minutes or until reduced ⅔. Using a wooden spoon, chop
spinach. Spoon spinach into prepared pie dish. Arrange potatoes over
spinach. Sprinkle with nutmeg. Season with salt and pepper.
In a small bowl, beat egg and milk. Pour over potatoes. Let stand 5
minutes. Bake in preheated oven 2 hours. Makes 4 servings.

Per serving: 300 kcal/18 g protein/8 g fat/43 g carbohydrate/12 g fiber

Leek Timbale

Photograph, page 100

1 lb. leeks, sliced	1 cup whole-wheat breadcrumbs
2 tablespoons butter or	1¼ cups low-fat milk
margarine	1 recipe Hot Sauce, Kosheri (omit
5 eggs	cumin and chili powder,
¼ cup shredded Gruyère cheese	page 76) or Mushroom Sauce,
⅛ teaspoon grated nutmeg	Buckwheat Noodles with
Salt	Mushroom Sauce (page 85)
Pepper	

Preheat oven to 350F (175C). Grease a mold or soufflé dish.
In a medium saucepan, cook leeks and butter or margarine over low
heat, covered, 5 to 8 minutes. Cool. In a blender, process leeks and eggs
to a purée. In large bowl, combine purée, Gruyère cheese and nutmeg.
Season with salt and pepper.
Pour breadcrumbs into prepared dish. Shake so breadcrumbs stick to
bottom and sides. Shake loose breadcrumbs into purée.
In a small saucepan, heat milk almost to boiling point. Pour slowly into
purée, beating continuously. Pour mixture slowly into mold or soufflé
dish. Do not disturb breadcrumbs.
Place mold or soufflé dish in a baking pan filled with boiling water. Bake
in preheated oven 45 minutes or until set firm. Remove from oven. Let
stand 5 minutes. Unmold on a platter. Make Hot Sauce or Mushroom
Sauce as directed. Pour Hot Sauce or Mushroom Sauce around edge of
timbale. Makes 4 servings.

Per serving: 275 kcal/15 g protein/16 g fat/19 g carbohydrate/5 g fiber

Pumpkin & Tomato Casserole $\boxed{V}$

2 lbs. tomatoes	2 tablespoons butter or
3 garlic cloves, minced	margarine
1 large bunch fresh basil,	1½ lbs. fresh pumpkin, cubed
chopped	Salt
1 tablespoon olive oil	Pepper

Preheat oven to 350F (175C). Grease a 13" × 9" baking dish.

In a large saucepan, cook tomatoes, garlic, basil and oil, covered, 10 minutes. Cool. Strain through a sieve. Reserve tomato sauce. Discard skins. In a large skillet, melt butter or margarine. Fry pumpkin 5 minutes. Add tomato sauce. Season with salt and pepper. Pour into prepared baking dish. Bake in preheated oven 15 minutes. Makes 4 servings.

Per serving: 140 kcal/3 g protein/9 g fat/13 g carbohydrate/7 g fiber

Winter Casserole $\boxed{V}$

1 lb. potatoes, peeled, chopped	1 tablespoon Dijon-style
5 cups vegetable stock (page 43)	mustard
2 tablespoons butter or	2 tablespoons butter or
margarine	margarine, softened
1 tablespoon olive oil	¼ cup all-purpose flour
1 lb. carrots, chopped	Salt
1 lb. turnips, chopped	Pepper
1 bunch celery, chopped	1 bunch fresh parsley, finely
⅔ cup shoyu soy sauce	chopped

Preheat oven to 350F (175C). Grease a 13" × 9" baking dish.

In a large saucepan, cook potatoes and vegetable stock 10 minutes. In prepared baking dish, heat butter or margarine and olive oil. Add carrots, turnips and celery. Cook 1 to 2 minutes. Add potatoes and vegetable stock. Mix in shoyu soy sauce and mustard. Bake in preheated oven 30 minutes.

In a small bowl, mix butter or margarine and flour to form a paste. Season casserole with salt and pepper. Add small amounts of flour paste to casserole, stirring vigorously, until sauce thickens. Stir in parsley. Makes 6 servings.

Per serving: 250 kcal/7 g protein/11 g fat/33 g carbohydrate/8 g fiber

FRUIT DISHES

The best and most healthful conclusion to a meal is fresh fruit, with nothing added. But sometimes our palates demand something more enticing. Certainly in summer when berries are in season, a range of fruit salads can hardly be beat. There are no recipes for fruit salads because they are created from the best of seasonal fruits. It is well to remember never to peel fruits and always to use them as fresh as possible. The other controversial issue is how much to sweeten. All sugars are equally bad for us in that they cause tooth decay and are a large contributory factor to obesity. Fresh ripe fruit should be sweet enough. If not, fruit salads can be marinated in apple juice or a little concentrated orange juice.

This section offers many recipes using dried apricots and other dried fruits. This is because dried apricots are a rich source of dietary fiber, minerals and vitamins. They are also astonishingly delicious and sweet. When buying dried fruits, go for the best. It pays to buy the most expensive, for a little goes a long way. Dried fruits also are a stunning combination with nuts as in the Syrian Fruit Salad (page 110).

Nectarines & Strawberries in Red Wine $\boxed{V}$

1 lb. strawberries, hulled   1 cup dry red wine
6 nectarines, halved, pitted

In a large bowl, combine strawberries and nectarines. Pour wine over fruit. Let stand 4 to 5 hours. Makes 6 servings.

Per serving: 110 kcal/2 g protein/negligible fat/18 g carbohydrate/4 g fiber

Marinated Oranges

6 large oranges   2 tablespoons apple juice
⅔ cup orange-flavored liqueur

Grate orange peel. Peel all pith from flesh. Slice thinly crosswise. In a medium bowl, layer orange slices. Sprinkle peel over top. Pour orange-flavored liqueur and apple juice over oranges. Let stand 4 to 5 hours. Refrigerate. Makes 4 servings.

Per serving: 170 kcal/2 g protein/negligible fat/30 g carbohydrate/4 g fiber

Brandied Apricots $\boxed{\text{V}}$

⅓ cup brown sugar   1 lb. dried apricots
⅔ cup water   1¼ cups brandy

In a small saucepan, boil sugar and water to make a syrup. In a sterilized jar with a tight-fitting lid, combine syrup and apricots. Pour brandy over apricots. Screw on lid of jar very tightly. Let stand in a cool dark place 1 month.

Once apricots have soaked up liquid, more brandy may need to be added. Makes 4 servings.

Per serving: 420 kcal/6 g protein/negligible fat/63 g carbohydrate/27 g fiber

Melon Stuffed with Raspberry Cream

1 lb. fresh raspberries   2 cantaloupes, halved, seeded,
1 cup Neufchâtel cheese   chilled
1 tablespoon honey, if desired

In a medium bowl, mix raspberries, cheese and honey, if desired. Spoon into cantaloupe cavity. Refrigerate 1 hour. Makes 4 servings.

Per serving: 155 kcal/13 g protein/3 g fat/21 g carbohydrate/10 g fiber

Syrian Fruit Salad

½ cup dried apricots   2 tablespooons golden raisins
½ cup dried figs   2 tablespoons slivered almonds
½ cup dried peaches   2 tablespoons chopped walnuts
⅓ cup prunes   2 tablespoons pine nuts
Water   2 tablespoons honey
2 tablespoons raisins   2 tablespoons rose water

In a large bowl, cover apricots, figs, peaches and prunes with water. Soak 8 to 10 hours. Drain; reserve liquid. Pit prunes. Chop all fruit. In a large bowl, combine reserved liquid, fruit, raisins, golden raisins, almonds, walnuts, pine nuts, honey and rose water. Let stand 24 hours. Makes 6 servings.

Per serving: 220 kcal/4 g protein/8 g fat/36 g carbohydrate/12 g fiber

Syrian Fruit Salad (*above*), Apricot & Ginger Tart (*center*, page 116), Melon Stuffed with Raspberry Cream (*below*)

Marinated Dried Fruits [V]

½ cup dried apricots
½ cup dried peaches
½ cup dried figs
1 tablespoon thawed frozen
   orange juice concentrate
⅔ cup ginger wine
⅔ cup brandy
Water

In a large bowl, combine apricots, peaches, figs, orange juice concentrate, ginger wine and brandy. Add enough water to cover fruit. Let stand 24 hours. Chop fruit coarsely; return to marinade. Let stand 24 hours. Makes 4 servings.

Per serving: 270 kcal/2 g protein/negligible fat/37 g carbohydrate/12 g fiber

Apple & Nut Salad

4 apples, cored, thinly sliced
½ cup chopped walnuts
½ cup slivered almonds
1 tablespoon honey
1 tablespoon walnut oil
1 tablespoon yogurt

In a large bowl, mix apples, walnuts and almonds. In a small bowl, mix honey, oil and yogurt. Drizzle over salad. Toss thoroughly. Makes 4 servings.

Per serving: 250 kcal/5 g protein/18 g fat/18 g carbohydrate/5 g fiber

Apricot & Almond Purée [V]

1½ cups dried apricots
Water
½ cup ground almonds
2 tablespoons butter or
   margarine
1 tablespoon honey, if desired
½ cup flaked almonds, toasted

In a medium bowl, cover apricots with water. Soak 8 to 10 hours. In a medium saucepan, simmer apricots and liquid 10 minutes. Cool. In a blender, process apricots and liquid, ground almonds, butter or margarine and honey, if desired, to a purée. Sprinkle flaked almonds over top. Makes 4 servings.

Per serving: 315 kcal/8 g protein/20 g fat/28 g carbohydrate/18 g fiber

---

Indian Mixed Pickle (*above*, page 121), Roquefort Cheesecake (*center*, page 118), Parsley Cheesecake (*below*, page 117)

Apricot & Walnut Fool

1¾ cups dried apricots
Water
¼ cup raisins
⅔ cup rum

⅔ cup dry sherry
1 cup Neufchâtel cheese
¾ cup chopped walnuts

In a medium bowl, cover apricots with water. Soak 8 to 10 hours. In a small bowl, combine raisins and rum. Soak 8 to 10 hours.

In a medium saucepan, simmer apricots and liquid 10 minutes. In a blender, process apricots and liquid, sherry and Neufchâtel cheese to a purée. Pour purée into a serving dish. Cover with raisins and rum. Sprinkle walnuts over top. Refrigerate 1 hour. Makes 4 servings.

Per serving: 450 kcal/16 g protein/14 g fat/38 g carbohydrate/17 g fiber

Baked Apples with Apricots $\boxed{V}$

8 dried apricots
4 large tart apples, cored
2 tablespoons butter or
  margarine

½ cup ground almonds
1 tablespoon honey, if desired

In a small bowl, cover apricots with water. Soak 8 to 10 hours.

Preheat oven to 400F (200C). In a small bowl, mix butter or margarine, almonds and honey, if desired. Chop apricots. Add to nut mixture. Fill center of each apple with apricot mixture. Arrange in an 8-inch-square baking dish. Bake in preheated oven 20 to 30 minutes. Makes 4 servings.

Per serving: 220 kcal/3 g protein/5 g fat/44 g carbohydrate/15 g fiber

Baked Apples with Lemon & Walnuts

4 large tart apples, cored
Grated peel and juice of 1 lemon
2 tablespoons butter or
  margarine
1 tablespoon honey, if desired

½ cup ground walnuts

To decorate:
4 walnut halves

Preheat oven to 400F (200C).

Arrange apples in an 8-inch-square baking dish. In a small bowl, mix lemon peel and juice, butter or margarine, honey if desired, and ground walnuts to a smooth paste. Fill center of apples with nut mixture. Bake in preheated oven 20 to 30 minutes. Decorate with walnut halves. Makes 4 servings.

Per serving: 220 kcal/2 g protein/12 g fat/28 g carbohydrate/7 g fiber

Peach Tart

¾ cup dried peaches
Water
1 (9-inch) Whole-Wheat Pastry
   shell, Zucchini Tart (page 65)

⅔ cup water
2 tablespoons brown sugar
4 fresh peaches, halved, pitted

In a small bowl, cover dried peaches with water. Soak 8 to 10 hours. Make pastry as directed. Cool. In a small saucepan, simmer peaches and liquid 10 minutes. Cool. In a blender, process peaches and liquid to a purée.

Fill pastry shell with purée. In a medium saucepan, cook water and sugar to make a syrup. Add fresh peaches. Cook 5 minutes. Using a slotted spoon, remove peaches from syrup. Arrange on top of tart. Glaze with syrup. Makes 6 servings.

Per serving: 260 kcal/4 g protein/10 g fat/41 g carbohydrate/5 g fiber

Spiced Fig Tart

1½ cups dried figs
Water
1 (9-inch) Whole-Wheat Pastry
   shell, Zucchini Tart (page 65)
⅔ cup dry white wine
⅛ teaspoon cloves
⅛ teaspoon mace

⅛ teaspoon ginger
⅛ teaspoon cinnamon
1 tablespoon raisins
1 tablespoon golden raisins
1 tablespoon currants
½ cup ground almonds
1 tablespoon blanched almonds

In a medium bowl. cover figs with water. Soak 8 to 10 hours. Make pastry shell as directed. Cool. In a medium saucepan, simmer figs and liquid, wine and spices 10 minutes. Cool. In a blender, process apricots and liquid, raisins, golden raisins, currants and ground almonds to a purée.

Fill pastry shell with purée. Arrange blanched almonds on top. Makes 6 servings.

Per serving: 295 kcal/5 g protein/13 g fat/38 g carbohydrate/9 g fiber

Apricot & Ginger Tart $\boxed{\text{V}}$

Photograph, page 111

1½ cups dried apricots
½ cup ground almonds
2 tablespoons butter or
  margarine

1 (9-inch) Whole-Wheat Pastry
  shell, Zucchini Tart (page 65)
½ cup preserved ginger in syrup

In a medium bowl, cover apricots with water. Soak 8 to 10 hours. Make pastry as directed. Cool. In a medium saucepan, simmer apricots and liquid 10 minutes. Cool. In a blender, process apricots and liquid, ground almonds and butter or margarine to a purée. Fill pastry shell with purée. Slice ginger. Top purée with overlapping slices of ginger. Drizzle syrup over top. Chill. Makes 6 servings.

Per serving: 380 kcal/5 g protein/19 g fat/52 g carbohydrate/8 g fiber

Apple & Chestnut Tart $\boxed{\text{V}}$

1 (9-inch) Whole-Wheat Pastry
  shell, Zucchini Tart (page 65)
1 (1-lb.) can chestnut purée
1 large tart apple, peeled, cored,
  sliced

3 tablespoons mixed candied peel
½ cup blanched almonds
Grated peel and juice of 1 lemon

Make pastry as directed. Cool. Preheat oven to 400F (200C).

Fill pastry shell with chestnut purée. Arrange apple slices over purée. Sprinkle mixed candied peel and almonds over top of apples. Sprinkle with lemon peel and juice. Bake in preheated oven 15 minutes. Makes 8 servings.

Per serving: 325 kcal/4 g protein/13 g fat/51 g carbohydrate/9 g fiber

CHEESES, SNACKS & PICKLES

Here are a few suggestions for ending a meal, though some may make a snack or light lunch. We too easily neglect the low-fat cheeses, finding them rather bland. Here are ways of brightening them up.

We tend to be too conservative in making pickles. Most vegetables take very kindly to being flavored in a pickling mixture with garlic and ginger. Malt vinegar is too strong a flavor, destroying the natural flavor of vegetables themselves. Instead, cider or wine vinegar should always be used.

Parsley Cheesecake

Photograph, page 112

3 tablespoons fresh parsley, finely
    chopped
1 cup ricotta cheese
Salt

Pepper
⅓ cup regular rolled oats,
    toasted

In a small bowl, mix parsley and ricotta cheese. Season with salt and pepper. Form cheese into a round cake. Roll in oats. Refrigerate. Makes 1 (8-oz.) cheesecake.

Total recipe: 615 kcal/22 g protein/58 g fat/2 g carbohydrate/5 g fiber

Chive Cheesecake

3 tablespoons fresh chives, finely
    chopped
1 cup ricotta cheese
Salt

Pepper
¼ cup buckwheat groats,
    toasted

In a small bowl, mix chives and ricotta cheese. Season with salt and pepper. Form cheese into a round cake. Roll in buckwheat groats. Refrigerate. Makes 1 (8-oz.) cheesecake.

Total recipe: 690 kcal/22 g protein/58 g fat/19 g carbohydrate/5 g fiber

Roquefort Cheesecake   *Photograph, page 112*

½ cup crumbled Roquefort
  cheese
1 cup ricotta cheese
3 tablespoons fresh mint, finely
  chopped

Freshly ground pepper
3 tablespoons sesame seeds,
  toasted

In a small bowl, mix Roquefort cheese, ricotta cheese and mint thoroughly. Season with pepper. Form cheese into a rounded cake. Roll cheese in sesame seeds. Refrigerate. Makes 1 (8-oz.) cheesecake.

Total recipe: 1010 kcal/37 g protein/93 g fat/7 g carbohydrate/1 g fiber

Cheesecake with Walnuts

1 tablespoon walnut oil
1 cup ricotta cheese
½ cup chopped walnuts

Salt
Pepper
2 tablespoons green peppercorns

In a small bowl, mix oil, ricotta cheese and walnuts thoroughly. Season with salt and pepper. Form cheese into a cake. Roll in green peppercorns. Makes 1 (8-oz.) cheesecake.

Total recipe: 1000 kcal/24 g protein/99 g fat/4 g carbohydrate/3 g fiber

Liptauer Cheese

½ cup ricotta cheese
½ cup Neufchâtel cheese
1 tablespoon paprika
1 bunch green onions, chopped
1 tablespoon capers

1 tablespoon chopped sweet
  pickles
Salt
Pepper

In a small bowl, mix ricotta cheese, Neufchâtel cheese, paprika, green onions, capers and sweet pickles. Season with salt and pepper. Refrigerate. Makes 1 cup cheese.

Total recipe: 435 kcal/26 g protein/34 g fat/7 g carbohydrate/2 g fiber

Bean Purée Toast

4 slices whole-wheat bread,
   toasted
6 tablespoons Navy Bean Dip
   (page 31)

8 slices mozzarella cheese
1 teaspoon paprika

Spread Navy Bean Dip on toasted bread. Broil 2 to 3 minutes. Place 2 slices of mozzarella cheese on each piece of toast. Broil until cheese melts. Sprinkle paprika on top of each slice. Makes 4 servings.

Per serving: 275 kcal/14 g protein/14 g fat/25 g carbohydrate/7 g fiber

Avocado Toast

6 tablespoons Avocado Sauce,
   Avocado Sauce & Fresh
   Vegetables (page 35)
4 slices whole-wheat bread,
   toasted

4 tomatoes, sliced
1 tablespoon capers

Spread Avocado Sauce on toasted bread. Top each piece with a tomato and a few capers. Broil 1 to 2 minutes. Makes 4 servings.

Per serving: 165 kcal/5 g protein/6 g fat/24 g carbohydrate/7 g fiber

Stuffed Mushrooms

4 large mushrooms, wiped clean
2 tablespoons butter or
   margarine
1 cup whole-wheat breadcrumbs
3 garlic cloves, minced
¼ cup cottage cheese

⅔ cup grated Parmesan cheese
3 tablespoons parsley, finely
   chopped
Salt
Pepper

Preheat oven to 400F (200C). Grease an 8-inch-square baking dish.
   Remove mushrooms stalks. If not too fibrous, chop finely. In a small saucepan, melt butter or margarine. Add mushroom stalks. Cook 1 to 2 minutes or until soft. In a medium bowl, mix mushroom stalks, breadcrumbs, garlic, cottage cheese, Parmesan cheese and parsley. Season with salt and pepper. Fill upturned mushrooms with stuffing. Arrange in prepared baking dish. Bake in preheated oven 10 minutes. Serve hot. Makes 4 servings.

Per serving: 185 kcal/9 g protein/13 g fat/9 g carbohydrate/3 g fiber

Parmesan Toast

1 cup grated Parmesan cheese
¾ cup shredded Gruyère cheese
¼ cup butter or margarine,
　softened

Salt
Pepper
4 slices whole-wheat bread,
　toasted

In a medium bowl, mix Parmesan cheese, Gruyère cheese and butter or margarine. Seaon with salt and pepper. Spread mixture on toasted bread. Broil until cheese melts and bubbles. Serve at once. Makes 4 servings.

Per serving: 385 kcal/18 g protein/26 g fat/21 g carbohydrate/4 g fiber

Macaroni Croquettes

1½ cups whole-wheat macaroni
2 tablespoons butter or
　margarine
¼ cup all-purpose flour
1¼ cups low-fat milk
½ cup shredded Cheddar cheese

Salt
Pepper
1 egg, beaten
1 cup whole-wheat breadcrumbs
Corn oil

In a large saucepan, cook macaroni in lightly salted boiling water 5 minutes or until tender but firm. Drain. Chop in small pieces. In a small saucepan, melt butter or margarine. Add flour to make a roux. Stir in milk gradually. Add cheese. Season with salt and pepper. Stir until thick. Remove from heat. Cool. Stir in chopped macaroni.

　Form mixture into small croquettes. Dip into beaten egg. Roll in breadcrumbs. In a medium skillet, heat oil. Fry croquettes until golden brown. Makes 4 servings.

Per serving: 490 kcal/18 g protein/23 g fat/56 g carbohydrate/8 g fiber

Pickled Onions   V

3 lbs. small pearl onions
2¼ cups water
¼ cup sea salt
4 cups cider vinegar

2 tablespoons pickling spice
½ cup peeled, grated fresh
　gingerroot
2 dried red chilis

In a large saucepan, blanch onions in boiling water 2 to 3 minutes. Peel onions. Dissolve salt in water. Soak onions in brine 24 hours. Drain. Sterilize a large glass jar with a tight fitting lid. Keep hot until needed.

　In a medium saucepan, heat vinegar. Add pickling spice, ginger and chilies. Pack onions in sterilized jar. Cover with vinegar and spices. Seal jar tightly. Store up to 6 months. Makes 3 lbs.

Total recipe: 315 kcal/12 g protein/negligible fat/71 g carbohydrate/18 g fiber

Indian Mixed Pickle [V]

Photograph, page 112

1 small red cabbage, sliced
1 small cauliflower, sliced
1 cucumber, cubed
½ lb. fresh green beans, trimmed
½ lb. small pearl onions, peeled
¼ cup sea salt
4 cups cider vinegar
5 garlic cloves, peeled, sliced
⅓ cup peeled sliced fresh gingerroot
1 teaspoon cloves
1 teaspoon coriander
1 teaspoon mustard seed
1 teaspoon black peppercorns
1 teaspoon cayenne pepper
1 tablespoon turmeric
1 tablespoon allspice

In a large bowl, combine cabbage, cauliflower, cucumber, green beans and onions. Sprinkle salt over vegetables. Let stand 24 hours.

Sterilize a large glass jar with a tight fitting lid. Keep hot until needed.

In a large saucepan, boil vinegar, garlic, ginger and all spices. Rinse vegetables under cold running water. Pat dry. Pack in sterilized glass jar. Pour vinegar and spices over vegetables. Seal jar very tightly. Store up to 6 months. Makes 3 lbs.

Total recipe: 440 kcal/50 g protein/negligible fat/62 g carbohydrate/59 g fiber

Pickled Beets [V]

3 lbs. small beets
4 cups wine or cider vinegar
⅓ cup peeled grated fresh gingerroot
1 head garlic, cloves peeled, halved
2 dried red chilies
1 teaspoon black peppercorns

Sterilize a large glass jar with a tight fitting lid. Keep hot until needed.

In a large saucepan, cover beets with water. Boil until tender. Cool. Peel beets. Pack in sterilized glass jar. In a large saucepan, bring vinegar, ginger, garlic, chilies and peppercorns to a boil. Pour over beets. Seal jar tightly. Store up to 6 months. Makes 3 lbs.

Total recipe: 600 kcal/24 g protein/negligible fat/134 g carbohydrate/34 g fiber

Peppers Pickled in Olive Oil $\boxed{V}$

2 red bell peppers, cored, seeded,
  quartered
2 green bell peppers, cored, seeded,
  quartered
1 head garlic, cloves peeled

1 tablespoon sea salt
1 teaspoon fresh thyme
1 teaspoon fresh marjoram
2½ cups olive oil

In a large bowl, combine peppers and garlic. Sprinkle with salt. Let stand 24 hours.

Sterilize a large glass jar with a tight fitting lid. Keep hot until needed.

Wash vegetables under cold running water. Pat dry. Pack in sterilized glass jar. Sprinkle herbs over vegetables. Pour olive oil over vegetables. Seal jar tightly. Store up to 6 months. Makes 2 lbs.

Total recipe: 5330 kcal/6 g protein/582 g fat/19 g carbohydrate/7 g fiber

Pickled Apricots $\boxed{V}$

1 lb. dried apricots
1 head garlic, cloves peeled
4 cups wine or cider vinegar
1 tablespoon allspice
1 teaspoon cloves

1 teaspoon black peppercorns
1 teaspoon green peppercorns
1 teaspoon coriander
1 teaspoon sea salt

In a large bowl, cover apricots with cold water. Let stand 24 hours. Drain.

Sterilize a large glass jar with a tight fitting lid. Keep hot until needed.

Pack apricots and garlic into sterilized glass jar. In a large saucepan, bring vinegar, all spices and salt to a boil. Pour vinegar over apricots and garlic. Seal jar tightly. Store up to 6 months. Makes 2 lbs.

Total recipe: 885 kcal/27 g protein/negligible fat/207 g carbohydrate/ 110 g fiber

ACKNOWLEDGMENTS

The recipes come from many sources which include classic French and Italian cooking. I am always in the debt of Elizabeth David and also her scholar successors, Jane Grigson and Claudia Roden. But there are other colleagues to whom I am grateful – especially Jocelyn Dimbleby, David Scott, Arabella Boxer and Natalie Hambro – for their cooking, though not always vegetarian, is full of imaginative ideas.

1986   CS

I am indebted to my wife for reading and commenting on the manuscript.

1986   TS

The publishers would like to acknowledge Peter Myers, who took the photographs, assisted by Neil Mersh, Mike Rose for art direction, Sue Russell for styling, and Jane Suthering for food preparation.

INDEX

Page numbers in *italic* refer to the illustrations.